The Bottom Lines 2017:
52 More Motivating
Lessons in Leadership

The Bottom Lines 2017: 52 More Motivating Lessons in Leadership

Tom Zender

Copyright © 2017 Tom Zender
All rights reserved.

ISBN: 1542446198
ISBN 13: 9781542446198
Library of Congress Control Number: 2017900377
CreateSpace Independent Publishing Platform
North Charleston, South Carolina

ENDORSEMENTS

I highly recommend that you buy this book, read this book, and share this book with others. Whether you're a new business owner or a seasoned pro, this book has much to offer. The *Bottom Lines 2017: 52 More Memorable Lessons in Leadership* is a fantastic go-to-book that is both grounding and inspirational for business leaders. Tom Zender has once again delivered a book that will positively impact your leadership skills, business results, and your bottom line.

Mary Hall is the Founder and CEO of "Culture Wise Consulting" – Helping companies build a better workplace and build a better world. www.culturewiseconsulting.com

■ ■ ■

Wow! There are people who claim to be an expert and an authority; and then there's the real deal, like my friend and mentor – Tom Zender. His latest work, *The Bottom Lines 2017: 52 More Memorable Lessons in Leadership* is another prime example of how gifted he is as a writer, philosopher and business analyst. Tom's keen sense of what it takes to be a high impact, confident, and inspiring leader is well illustrated in his words, his phrasing, and examples shared in his latest book. Anyone looking for a great read and wants to capture tips and techniques from a true Master of Leadership Skills, you owe it to yourself to pick up a copy for yourself – and a few of your close friends and business associates.

Mike Hayashi, M.Ed. *is the "Owner of Take Control Self Defense" and has provided Corporate Seminars for over 500 companies, agencies, and Universities in 27 States and 4 Countries. With more than 500,000 trained in Personal Security and How to Be a Triple-P Professional Speaker (including Tom Zender), Mike has worked with leaders in The Fortune 500: IBM, Apple, AT&T, Blue Cross/Blue Shield, American Airlines, and The Four Seasons. He Co-Authored a Best-Seller with Dr. Wayne Dyer & Tony Robbins and was nominated for an Emmy. (480) 221- 0044. TakeControlSelfDefense.com*

. . .

I have known Tom Zender for many years and have seen his transformation into a successful leader. This fourth book of Tom's, *The Bottom Lines 2017: 52 More Memorable Lessons in Leadership*, is filled with his real-world experiences as a true business leader. Real stuff. The book bears his wisdom, practical application, and his easy to read and remember style of writing. Tom is a master leader and demonstrates it in this book. Thank you, Tom!

Dr. Fred Zook, Ed.D., is the former President of Ottawa University. As the leader of Ottawa's Phoenix campus, he grew the institution from less than 100 students to several thousand and three campuses in the Phoenix area.

DEDICATION

The Bottom Lines 2017: 52 More Memorable Lessons in Leadership is dedicated to the generous CEO's and business mentors who have enriched my career by sharing their wisdom, providing their unselfish guidance, and by giving their steadfast devotion to my success. I deeply thank you, always.

Also, this book is dedicated to the readers of my weekly column, **Leadership Lessons**, in the digital edition of the *Phoenix Business Journal*. In particular, their Chief Editor, Ilana Lowery, her Digital Editor, Tim Gallen, and their Publisher, Ray Schey, opened the door to give me the privilege of writing about the key element of all businesses – leadership.

And, not to forget my 16-year-old cat, Angel, my faithful Muse who inspired me in writing all of my books, including this one.

As always, I am indebted to my wife, Dr. Wendy Zender, Ph.D., and so many business friends who have supported me in creating *The Bottom Lines* series of books.

TABLE OF CONTENTS

	Endorsements ·v
	Foreword ·xv
	Preface · xix
	Acknowledgements · · · · · · · · · · · · · · · xxi
	About the Author · · · · · · · · · · · · · · · · xxiii
Leadership Lesson 1	There ain't no silver bullet marketing (really) · · · · · · · · · · · · · · · · · · · 1
Leadership Lesson 2	Leadership, ideas, and the alchemy of operations · · · · · · · · · · · · · · · 5
Leadership Lesson 3	What is your Listen/Talk Ratio? Good leaders listen up · · · · · · · · · · · · · · · · · · · 9
Leadership Lesson 4	Intrapreneurship: Learn how top leaders capture creativity within · · · · · · ·12
Leadership Lesson 5	Rocky road to success: How small business leaders drive and thrive · · · · · ·16
Leadership Lesson 6	Excellence vs. perfection: Smart leaders get it · · · · · · · · · · · · · · · · · ·19
Leadership Lesson 7	Fire in the attic: How entrepreneurial leaders think · 22
Leadership Lesson 8	Successful leadership: Aligning plans, people, and assets · · · · · · · · · · · 25

Leadership Lesson 9	Company culture, legacy leaders, and sustainable success	28
Leadership Lesson 10	The five pillars of leadership for successful projects	32
Leadership Lesson 11	Advanced marketing: Who is the customer of your customer?	36
Leadership Lesson 12	Here's how leaders set boundaries for others (and themselves)	39
Leadership Lesson 13	Persistence and leadership: Busting through barriers to success	43
Leadership Lesson 14	How nimble leaders cure sick businesses: A five-step turnaround	47
Leadership Lesson 15	Soul of the leader: Essence of the organization	51
Leadership Lesson 16	This is why great leaders choose great CFO's	55
Leadership Lesson 17	Leadership and the great computer burial ground	59
Leadership Lesson 18	Why "no strings attached" leadership succeeds	63
Leadership Lesson 19	Find out how leaders handle conflicts effectively	67
Leadership Lesson 20	Do you have it in you to be a real leader?	70
Leadership Lesson 21	Discover why "mindfulness" is key to legacy leadership	74
Leadership Lesson 22	How learning leaders build learning organizations	78
Leadership Lesson 23	Why you need to stamp out "scope creep"	82
Leadership Lesson 24	What is the "why" of your leadership?	86

Leadership Lesson 25	You forgot what? The crucial business of follow-up	90
Leadership Lesson 26	Plan B: How to cut risks with parallel strategies	94
Leadership Lesson 27	When should good leaders demand good due diligence?	98
Leadership Lesson 28	How to clean up a toxic organization	101
Leadership Lesson 29	Discover the power of serendipitous leadership	105
Leadership Lesson 30	What do you know about Theory M leadership?	108
Leadership Lesson 31	Three Steps to achieving Legacy Leadership	111
Leadership Lesson 32	How to open the gift of a bad decision	114
Leadership Lesson 33	How a leadership reboot can help your organization	117
Leadership Lesson 34	Why "anticipated satisfaction" is the core of great marketing	121
Leadership Lesson 35	Employees: Burn and churn, or train and retain?	125
Leadership Lesson 36	Why authenticity is the irresistible attraction of great business leaders	129
Leadership Lesson 37	See how clarity is the lens of leadership	133
Leadership Lesson 38	Five paths to profits from audacious value strategies	136
Leadership Lesson 39	Why breaking bread is so good for business	140
Leadership Lesson 40	How to avoid the customers you never want	144

Leadership Lesson 41	How do successful leaders start their mornings?	147
Leadership Lesson 42	The art and science of gratitude in business	151
Leadership Lesson 43	Bye-bye business plan, hello business model	155
Leadership Lesson 44	Why context is the framework for successful leadership	159
Leadership Lesson 45	Improvisation: When your plan isn't working	163
Leadership Lesson 46	Business bully, people manipulator, or positive influencer?	167
Leadership Lesson 47	Synchronicity in business: Why good things happen for no reason	171
Leadership Lesson 48	The magic of music in our workplaces	174
Leadership Lesson 49	Who muzzled word of mouth marketing?	178
Leadership Lesson 50	Important stuff to know about goals and objectives	181
Leadership Lesson 51	When and how to fire yourself	185
Leadership Lesson 52	How great managers can become great leaders	189
	How to Order More Books	193

FOREWORD

I have the privilege of counting Tom Zender as a friend, and the good fortune of having received some of his business wisdom. But in this book, you will garner so much more – 52 short, readable chapters covering leadership lessons that all business owners or managers should know.

The first thing you will notice is that Tom's approach is both "forest" and "trees." Rather than simply start with specific advice as so many other business books do, Tom first gives you an overview of the forest, the 5,000-foot view of the specific topic so that you may properly understand the challenges any leader faces applying the ideas to come. As a university professor of marketing, I've seen too many trade and textbooks that make it seem easy – just apply these rules or take these steps, and success will be yours. Tom gently throws a bucket of water on that idea, cautioning the reader that nothing is easy and little is guaranteed. As he says, you will never do it perfectly: "Create good value, not perfect failures."

One aspect of this book which appeals to most readers is the length of the chapters. They are "bite-sized," perfect for reading any time you have a few moments to spare. You'll be able to read the complete Lesson. That will make it easier to understand, remember and apply to your work. You can also open it to any random chapter that strikes your interest, each is self-contained and need not be read in any order.

Application is another strong point of each Lesson you will read. Understanding how to apply the lessons is an integral part of each chapter, and you'll also get a quick take-away at the end of the Lesson, making it easier for you to capture the essence of Tom's advice.

Readers of Tom's prior book, *The Bottom Lines 2016* (highly recommended!), commented on how easy the style of writing was, how it was almost like Tom was sitting next to them talking about his ideas. Tom, like many good writers, tries to create a voice inside his readers' heads, one that seems to naturally flow from idea to idea, linking them together into a coherent chain that is both memorable and easy to understand.

Tom has provided a book valuable to young start-up CEOs and seasoned business veterans, to those in the C-Suite and those who aspire to leadership. Some leaders may be born, but most leaders are made. They often learn by trial-and-error – unless they are lucky enough to come across Tom Zender, who can reduce both their trial and error as he educates them on how to become a great leader. Enjoy your journey and this book!

Dr. Gary Witt is a marketing psychologist and head of Marketing Psychology, LLC, a consulting firm in Scottsdale, AZ specializing in the analysis and application of buyer motivation to sales and marketing. He also teaches marketing, psychology, and communication at several universities.

PREFACE

I am a Professional CEO Mentor. I continuously meet great leaders in my work, learning valuable lessons along the way. During my business career, I have collected hundreds of business lessons from my mentors, leaders, clients, and others. These teachings are brief, simple, powerful. And immediately useful.

The Bottom Lines 2017 is devoted to sharing more of the best lessons I have learned with my readers – a wide audience of business people: leaders, managers, and you.

Rather than the typical laborious business writings that we encounter, I write in a more conversational way – because I find that business wisdom is easier and more interesting to read and remember. Brevity counts. So does a touch of humor.

My business path began with General Electric and Honeywell, and moved through midsize and startup companies, and a global nonprofit organization. My leadership roles included CEO, senior VP, and board member in Fortune 500, NASDAQ, Toronto Stock Exchange, and other companies.

Today I am a professional CEO Mentor & Business Coach. Additionally, I mentor Arizona State University faculty members and students who have startup businesses, as well as serving the Maricopa County Community College District. And, I write a weekly column, *Leadership Lesson*, for the Phoenix Business Journal.

I have had a taste of everything on the broad buffet of business. Mostly satisfying. But with some occasional heartburn, too!

The Bottom Lines 2017 includes a wide variety of lessons from different business functions. Above all, they are useful for building better business. Proven stuff.

Now, you can read and benefit from such penetrating insights as:

- *Do you have it in you to be a real leader?*
- *Soul of the leader: Essence of the organization*
- *Three steps to achieving Legacy Leadership*
- *Discover the power of serendipitous leadership*
- *What is your Listen/Talk Ratio? Good leaders listen up*

Each lesson ends with a short summary. Here is the one for *Three steps to achieving Legacy Leadership*:

The Bottom Lines

Decide now. What is the enduring legacy that you will leave for our world? Not your values, personality, or reputation. Leave three things: indelible visions, durable teams, and stellar products. These serve others. For good.

ACKNOWLEDGEMENTS

Thank you, all of my durable business mentors at General Electric, Honeywell, Ottawa University, University of California at Irvine, and many others.

I am grateful to my mentors who taught me to mentor others as my way of giving away what I learned.

And, yes, I thank my "anti-mentors" who unconsciously convinced me about many attitudes and behaviors that I do not want to emulate. Ever.

I thank hundreds of business writers who have produced the mass of books, articles, columns, and other publications that have so positively influenced me.

Thank you so very much to many business and personal friends for giving me ongoing support to bring *The Bottom Lines Series* of books to business readers who seek new ways to improve their leadership skills.

Tom Zender

Thank you to the team at CreateSpace, Kindle Direct Publishing, and Amazon for their focused and expert assistance to help me to transform this book, and the other books in this series, from a vision into a reality.

Above all, I am forever grateful to my wife, chief supporter, and editor, Dr. Wendy Zender, Ph.D., University of Southern California. Wendy is gifted in helping me transform good ideas into something readable and useful. She should be. She is a graduate university professor who reads a continuous stream of doctoral level theses from her students. I think I am one of them!

ABOUT THE AUTHOR

Tom Zender is a Professional CEO Mentor in Phoenix, Arizona.

He held leadership roles at General Electric and Honeywell, and has been a senior vice president in publicly held corporations, New York Stock Exchange and NASDAQ listed. Tom was the CEO of a startup technology company and he was president and CEO of a global nonprofit that serves over two million people globally.

His corporate board experience includes NASDAQ, Toronto Stock Exchange, and OTC listed public companies. Tom held nonprofit board positions with Ottawa University and the Forum for Corporate Directors.

In his CEO and senior vice president roles he held profit and loss responsibility for every business function.

Tom writes a weekly column, **Leadership Lesson**, for the Phoenix Business Journal, mentors faculty and students who have startup businesses at Arizona State University, and is an advisor to

Paradise Valley Community College. And, he serves the Maricopa County Community College District's Center for Entrepreneurial Innovation (CEI).

He has spoken to business audiences of over 1,000 people in more than 30 countries.

Tom Zender is a graduate of Ottawa University with a B.A. in Business in focus areas of Leadership, Marketing, and Information Technology.

His first two published books were Amazon bestseller e-books about business ethics:

- *God Goes to Work* was among the top ten e-books in business ethics listed by Amazon.com. Published in 2010 by John Wiley & Sons, it was widely distributed in the United States, Canada, the UK, Australia, and India.
- *One-Minute Meditations at Work*. Published in 2011 by Hay House/Balboa Press, it was among the top 5% of all e-books sold by Amazon.com.

His third book, *The Bottom Lines 2016: 52 Unforgettable Lessons in Leadership,* is a prequel to this book – and part of the growing *The Bottom Lines Series* of books.

Tom's email address is tomzender@me.com and his website is www.tomzender.com

LEADERSHIP LESSON 1

THERE AIN'T NO SILVER BULLET MARKETING (REALLY)

One shot marketing. The perfect website, or press release, or advertisement, or LinkedIn posting will create a skyrocket success for this new product. One tradeshow, or mention by a celebrity, or sponsoring one event will make this new service take off like a shot. Not.

"The Field of Dreams" movie's now famous quote, *"Build it and they will come,"* turns out be a bad dream – and poor judgment in marketing.

There is no single-solution (the silver bullet) for effective marketing. We have raced from fad-to-fad in order to gain a marketing foothold. Only to slide off the slippery slope of instant gratification. Ooooops.

Don't shoot from the hip

There are a lot of choices in marketing. Rather than taking random shots, think strategy. What are your best marketing choices based upon: who are the intended customers, where are they, what are their anticipated satisfiers, and what are your uniqueness's?

Better aim: what are the pricing drivers, how important are support and service, what do they want to know and why?

Most of all, what forms of media appeal to your audience? Better find out.

Bang for the buck

So where will you spend your marketing money? Here are some of the channels you can utilize:

<u>Social media</u> – building content about products and services, and distributing it via LinkedIn and other social media engines. Also, place ads in social media sites.

<u>Targeted advertising</u> – running ads in electronic magazines and news outlets. These ads can link to your website and social media sites to gain more visibility.

<u>Trade shows</u> – having a booth with presentations, demonstrations, and promotional materials. And, providing knowledgeable speakers to participate in forums and panels.

<u>Event sponsorship</u> – financially support an event of interest to your buying audience. Typically, you can have some presentation and demonstration space, too.

Published e-newsletters – for a small price, you can distribute digital newsletters with educational, informative, and promotional content. A digital "infomercial."

TV ads – sometimes pricey, but well targeted programming can deliver powerful messages to very large audiences. For some campaigns, radio is very effective.

Lead generation – often using telephones, a variety of services will find prospective customers, pre-sell your product, and then set up appointments for your sales team.

Strategy first. Then mix it up. Build a campaign with an optimum, selected blend of marketing tools. Shoot at several targets simultaneously. Because some methods will work better than others, but we are never sure ahead of time.

"Honestly, I don't have a silver-bullet answer."

– Victor Murphy, National Weather Service forecaster

Shotgun approach works

Coca-Cola has introduced recently another new product – Coke Life, a healthier option to high-sugar drinks.

Coke has used some 7,000 national outdoor areas with digital screen ads, billboards, and ads on city busses - plus point of sale, digital and print promotions, and a contest to win prizes. Interestingly, TV is not being used.

Based upon social media buzz, this launch is being successful. It appears to be an excellent integrated marketing campaign. Good shot.

The bottom lines
No silver bullet. No single shot. Not in marketing. Ask the questions that will answer: who are your customers, what do they want, and in what media will they notice the information they need? Then implement an optimized multi-channel marketing program that hits all targets. More bangs for your bucks.

LEADERSHIP LESSON 2

LEADERSHIP, IDEAS, AND THE ALCHEMY OF OPERATIONS

Great ideas. Intentions for new products and services. But an intention without action is just an intention. The alchemists of long ago attempted sorcery to transform ideas into reality. Such as turning lead into gold. They didn't sit around with ideas. They took action to implement them.

Good leaders know that nothing happens until something happens. Their alchemists of today are the Chief Operating Officer (COO) and teams. Turning visions into products of worth. With brilliant organization and hard work.

"Leaders must invoke an alchemy of great vision."

– HENRY KISSINGER, FORMER U.S. SECRETARY OF STATE

Lost gold

Surveys show that most organizations commercialize only one out of five good ideas. And only one in eight leaders believe that their companies are adept at converting good ideas into commercial products. Even the highly innovative organizations convert less than 60% of the best ideas.

There are "idea people" and "implementer people." Leaders who understand this free the idea teams to be their creative best. And the implementers can delight in using their operational alchemy to commercialize enticing new products. Win-win.

A faster path to products and profits.

Enter the magician

In many organizations the COO is charged with the activity of converting ideas into commercialized goods and services. The COO typically reports to the Chief Executive Officer (CEO) of the company. COO's lead the active chain of functions that bring ideas to market:

<u>Engineering and Development</u> – designing, prototyping, testing, modifying, documenting, for the new products. Preparing for manufacturing/production.

<u>Manufacturing</u> – ordering parts, establishing assembly lines, creating processes, providing quality assurance, staffing, and more. Scaling up the production process.

Marketing and Sales – devising go-to-market strategies, advertising, public relations, website, sales materials, sales plans, staffing, management. Order processing.

Customer Service – preparing for, and providing, customer installations, training, maintenance, spare parts, diagnostics. Ongoing support.

Frequently, the COO also has responsibility for Facilities for the entire company. There are other departments that do not report to the COO, but provide support for operations. These include HR and Accounting/Finance. But the operations team has the responsibility to make the core business run successfully. The Hot Seat.

The magic wand
What are the key qualities of good Chief Operating Officers? Here are some answers from various companies: shares vision with the board and CEO; respected by the team; obsessed with action management; passion for new methods and tools; IT smart; are willing to do anything they ask their people to do.

Great COO's are compulsive organizers for teamwork and efficiency; they strive for excellence in all things; they have strong communication skills; are highly detailed and steeped in operational data; they are excellent mentors and coaches for their team; they are passionate about results. They are process junkies.

Wizards!

A tasty example
The COO of Yummly is Brian Witlin. Yummly is a post-startup company that provides online personalized recipes and food management services to over 14 million people globally. Brian notes, "I am responsible for our product roadmap, and translating the company's vision into reality. My favorite part of my daily duties is interacting with my co-workers."

The bottom lines
No magic. Good leaders know that transforming great ideas into great products requires great operations. And strong COO's are key to rapid and successful time-to-market products and profits. COO's are the alchemists of action. Wizards that work.

LEADERSHIP LESSON 3

WHAT IS YOUR LISTEN/TALK RATIO? GOOD LEADERS LISTEN UP

All ears. Ever hear of the "Listen/Talk Ratio?" It is important to understand and practice by leaders, managers, and everyone. The more we talk, the less we listen. And it is in listening that we can learn important things. Something that will make or break a team, organization, or business. Great leaders listen more, talk less.

We are a nation of talkers. Culturally, we are driven from childhood on to talk. Our first words, learning how to read aloud, courses in speaking, debate, and making presentations. But we receive little education in how to listen effectively.

> *"If we were supposed to talk more than we listen, we would have two tongues and one ear."*
>
> — MARK TWAIN, AUTHOR AND HUMORIST

Research this

A 2011 *Harvard Business Review* article suggests that we should listen ten times more than we talk. 10:1, especially with customers. The more we learn the better we can serve them. Even if we listen twice as much as we talk, a Talk/Listen Ratio of 2:1, we are the gainers.

If we do not focus on what someone else is saying we miss an opportunity to be receptive, to learn, to be involved deeply, to show respect. And, to be respected.

We only learn from ourselves when we talk incessantly, but we learn from others when we listen attentively.

Listening vs. hearing

Hearing enables listening. Hearing is sensory, listening is mental. Hearing is involuntary, listening is active. Hearing is automatic, listening is purposeful. Hearing without listening is like talking without saying anything. Get the important difference?

Silence, too, is a form of listening. Remember Simon and Garfunkel's famous song, "The Sound of Silence." Silence is a language without words.

If you are hearing, but not listening, you might miss something. Such as your job.

Clean out your ears

Stop talking. Stop hearing words. Instead listen to the spoken message. Turn on your "record button." Here are some effective ways to be a better in-person listener (and use some of these in phone calls, too):

- Make eye contact with whoever is talking.
- Show interest with your posture.
- Remove all distractions.
- Take mental and written notes.
- Indicate that you are listening by periodically nodding your head.
- Prompt the speaker with an occasional question, e.g., "What happened next?"
- Don't consider what you might say – just listen.
- Let go of all stray thoughts and keep listening.
- Practice patience, remain open-minded, avoid assumptions.
- Allow speakers to finish completely prior to you saying anything.

Why will this work? Simple. We humans can listen much faster than we speak. Research suggests that we usually listen and comprehend at 300 WPM (words per minute) while a typical presenter speaks at 100 WPM. Easy listening.

Enough is enough

What to do when the speaker has said too much or run out the clock? Simply interrupt politely at some point and say, "Thank you. I would like hear from some others, as well." Or, "We are running out of time and I would like to share my thoughts, too." Or, "Can we resume this later?"

The bottom lines

Listen up. Raise your Listen/Talk Ratio. Stop hearing words and start listening to the messages that can boost your business. The speaker feels respected and you can learn valuable information. Be a better leader. Listen better.

LEADERSHIP LESSON 4

INTRAPRENEURSHIP: LEARN HOW TOP LEADERS CAPTURE CREATIVITY WITHIN

You mean entrepreneurship? Nope. Intrapreneurship. Stop thinking that entrepreneurs are associated only with startups. Fact: most entrepreneurs work within established large, midsize, and small businesses. Working inside. Call them "intrapreneurs." The inventors within enlightened enterprises. There were 300,000 new patents issued by the United States in 2015. Most of them came from intrapreneurs. Not entrepreneurs.

Case in point. IBM was granted the most patents again in 23 continuous years, with 7,355 patents issued. Samsung was second with 5,072 and Canon number 3 with 4,134 patents. These are large, established companies with significant numbers of intrapreneurs within their organizations.

Yes, we love entrepreneurs – but give the intrapreneurs a hug, too.

The Bottom Lines 2017: 52 More Motivating Lessons in Leadership

Post it

Post-Its, that is. The famous "sticky note." A classic example of intrapreneurship at work. In 1974 a 3M engineer, Arthur Fry, spotted a spinoff idea from another 3M project. A special adhesive project was failing – but the resulting glue had a slight tacky quality.

Fry tried some of the failed substance to stick a note in his hymnal. It worked. And it was removable easily. The initial yellow color was from a piece of scrap paper in his 3M lab. This discovery became a major product. 3M Post-It Notes.

3M's compensation for engineers includes innovation bonuses. And these scientists can spend up to 15% of their time pursuing their own choice to for new opportunities. By "tinkering."

Internal incubators

While university and other external incubators are available for entrepreneurs to ignite an array of new businesses, the intrapreneurs have their labs, too. Internally.

"Skunkworks." That is the name that Lockheed gave to a separate facility with a special staff of engineers and an isolated budget to rapidly develop exotic, new, "can't be done" aircraft. Such as the SR-71 Blackbird flying at three times the speed of sound. In 1964.

Thomas Edison had his Menlo Park Lab, where he invented the light bulb. And entire new industries, including the electric power grid and General Electric. Hundreds of companies now have intrapreneurial incubators.

A new league

The League of Intrapreneurs, http://www.leagueofintrapreneurs.com, is a worldwide group that unifies and supports intrapreneurship. The League creates forums where intrapreneurs meet, swap stories, and help each other.

Barclays, Deloitte, and other companies have instituted programs to boost internal innovation. Education and support is provided to expand the spirit of intrapreneurship.

The real intrapreneurs know that they can significantly impact the future of their employers without the risks of being an external entrepreneur. Win-win.

Feeding the hungry

Real intrapreneurs have a drive to help. They are at their best when leaders give them the resources they need to succeed. Here are critical support areas that will help them:

- Freedom to fail – allow them to make mistakes on their way to success.
- Rewards for success – give them recognition and benefits of some kind.
- Fast and flexible culture – intrapreneurs do not succeed in slow, rigid environments.

> "The creative mind doesn't have to have the whole pattern; it can have just a little piece and be able to envision the whole picture in completion."
>
> – ARTHUR FRY, 3M ENGINEER.

The bottom lines

Intrapreneuers. The entrepreneurs within existing companies, large and small. They are driven to help their employers invent streams of new products. And services. Recognize them and give them strong support. They are creating the future. Now.

LEADERSHIP LESSON 5

ROCKY ROAD TO SUCCESS: HOW SMALL BUSINESS LEADERS DRIVE AND THRIVE

Beneath the corporate freeway. While big media pays big attention to big companies, there is an underground road that drives a flow new jobs. Small businesses. 75% of new jobs in America are provided by small businesses - 50% of people who work. Not small at all.

Women, too. There are now more than 10 million women-owned businesses, 35% of all small businesses. And they are growing at over 25% per year – faster than men-owned businesses. More jobs.

And not just jobs. Value. *"If we look at the American economy, who's really creating value? It's the small businesses."*

– Robert Herjavec, business leader.

Boulders on the road
Small business leaders face very low odds of success. Capital is scarce, competition is plentiful, profits are slim, and getting started takes enormous energy and time. It is a challenge to find reliable employees and pay them reasonably. And then keep them.

Government regulations, banking laws, tax burdens, insurance requirements, and HR rules are big rocks along the path. There is no straight freeway – no one solution. It takes high horsepower to accelerate growth, keep going, and reach sustainable success.

But the winners of the race grow, hire, prosper. And say it was all worth the ride.

Where is the fuel?
Small business leaders have many moving parts that work together – at times with a smooth sound, and sometimes with a crunchy clatter. Here are some leadership qualities in successful post-startup businesses:

1. Allow mistakes – everyone makes them. Learn from them, be resilient, and move on. And pass the learning on to others, internal and external. But repeated mistakes don't count. Ever.
2. Listen well – there is great wisdom in know what is happening with the team. There is power in asking meaningful questions, too. Make sure your "talk/listen ratio" is at least 50/50, if not skewed more to listening.

3. Hire smart – attract and retain those who are smarter than you. Invite the team to help hire great people. Reward them with as much recognition, cash, and benefits as you can. Include them in the monetary successes of the business.
4. Dream forward – paint the picture of how the business will look downstream and keep communicating it to all. Big dreams attract big people who want to share in the dream. They will help realize it with you.
5. Challenge everyone – in a professional way. Assign responsibilities clearly, hold everyone accountable for results, and delegate authority to accomplish goals. Entrust and empower the team, and they will overwhelm you with success.
6. Form relationships – within the team and outside with customers, vendors, and the community. Think long term relationships. Those that will help you accelerate growth and reach sustainable success. The long haul.
7. Create culture – an overarching responsibility of the small business leader. Done best by demonstration of the core values held by the leader. Positive culture builds trust, teamwork, and resiliency. Negative culture creates an energy that smothers success.

> *"In America, small business is a big deal."*
>
> – BOB BEAUPREZ, RANCHER, AUTHOR, POLITICIAN.

The bottom lines

Small is big. Small businesses are the roadways of our economy. Job creation, profits, value. Barriers are huge, but real leaders ride over them. Practice the qualities of adept small business leaders. Accelerate growth and reach sustainable success. Go faster.

LEADERSHIP LESSON 6

EXCELLENCE VS. PERFECTION: SMART LEADERS GET IT

Never good enough. Perfectionism. A seemingly good thing can be a pitfall in the path of progress. A cause of late to market, increased pricing, poor profits. Excellence is the alternative to perfection – good enough for success, but not overdone. Like beauty, perfection is in the eye of the beholder. And some beholders are blind.

Ergo, how much more time, energy, and cost should we spend to move from excellent to perfect? What is the cost of perfection when "perfect" is so illusory?

"Have no fear of perfection, you'll never reach it."

– Salvador Dali

Question and answer time

Question: "How will we know when we have reached a point of excellence?" Answer: "When we have pre-defined it." A stated standard of excellence. In other words, we decide ahead of time when we will reach a point of sufficient goodness or value.

This value is our desired combination of quality, cost, price, function, timing, reproducibility, serviceability, and other factors to which we can say, "Good enough!"

This does not mean that we stop looking for excellence, but that we pursue it as a continuum. The Japanese taught us a great concept, "kaizen." It simply means "continuous improvement." Kaizen has been the backbone of their auto industry. A lesson learned by the American automotive producers. The hard way.

Pareto knows

Pareto's Principle, otherwise known as the 80/20 rule, was developed by a management consultant named Joseph Juran. His research proposes that 80% of the effects generally come from 20% of the causes. He named his idea after Vilfredo Pareto, an Italian economist.

Pareto observed what become a somewhat universal idea of effort vs. value:

- 80% of Italian land was owned by 20% of the population.
- 80% of the peas were produced by 20% of the pods.
- Most importantly, 80% of the value is gained with 20% of the initial effort, and extended periods of time may pass before any more improvement is noted.

The Law of Diminishing Returns works, too. At some point, more effort isn't worth it.

Establishing excellence
Here are some effective ways to pre-determine acceptable levels of excellence:

1. Lay out a team agreement that defines the planned Scope and Limits of a project or process. Beware of "Scope Creep" – unapproved additions to the plan – which can bloat the value of the venture.
2. Define Roles and Responsibilities carefully. Document and communicate to everyone and gain agreement.
3. Lay out the Process to go from start to finish and use the team to develop it. This is another critical tool to make known for all those involved.
4. What Resources will be needed? Budget them and gain all the approvals needed. Have a good finance and accounting person help and monitor.
5. Deliverables: at the end of the project (or phase of a project) exactly what will be delivered to whom? This definitively describes how we will know how we are done.
6. These five areas are the essence of describing when we have achieved our own definition of excellence. Good value.

The bottom lines
Drive for perfection? You could be overdoing it, wasting time and money. Strive for excellence. Most of the time, 20% of our effort yields 80% of our result. And, we get to define and implement excellence. Create good value. Not perfect failures.

LEADERSHIP LESSON 7

FIRE IN THE ATTIC: HOW ENTREPRENEURIAL LEADERS THINK

Up in the brain. Something is burning. It is a new idea that has gone from a pilot light of imagination to a blaze of creativity in action. The enterprising entrepreneur has found a new niche in ever-changing markets. The response is moving into plans and products. The entrepreneur sees an opportunity with vision. They are off and running. Fast.

Plus, the entrepreneur of today also is a clever creator of new leadership principles and practices. Like flexible hours.

> *"The entrepreneur always searches for change, responds to it, and exploits it as an opportunity."*
>
> – PETER DRUCKER, MANAGEMENT CONSULTANT, EDUCATOR, AND AUTHOR.

The moving parts
What are the most common qualities of successful entrepreneurial leaders?

The Bottom Lines 2017: 52 More Motivating Lessons in Leadership

1. Passion fuels them and they live the coffee-cup mantra of, "Do what you love, and love what you do." Thomas Edison would not have conducted 10,000 experiments to create the light bulb if he had disliked his work.
2. Focus is the foundation of their seriousness - they are unmoved by negative people and events. The Wright brothers lived through the winds of "it cannot be done" to birth our 500 mile per hour jet travels around the world.
3. Planning is important for products, services, financing, strategy, business plans, and more. General Dwight Eisenhower's planning for the World War II D-Day invasion of Hitler-held Europe reversed a potential global disaster.
4. Cash flow management is not an accident, and entrepreneurial leaders create and obtain as much cash as possible. No wonder that Apple Computer now has $200 billion cash for opportunities and "rainy days."
5. Employees are a precious asset and are hired, cultivated, and retained with great care. Southwest Airlines built a fast growth, highly profitable business by caring for employees, who care for customers – profits soared.
6. Customer care from first contact, through the selling process, delivery, training, and ongoing support is the core of great new companies and industries. Amazon lives this and enjoys stunning growth and profits.
7. Persistence in the face of all odds over the long term carries most entrepreneurs through the agonies of starting and growing significant new businesses. Henry Ford had three failed auto companies before starting Ford Motor Company.

There are many more characteristics of entrepreneurial leaders for success, including: working through ambiguity, steadfast belief in themselves, self-care to manage stress, "turn-on-a-dime" flexibility. And a willingness to break rules and conventions, which is required to successfully start a new business. In the first place.

Inventing new leadership

Wait. The new entrepreneurs are in the laboratories of leadership as well. They have created contemporary leadership practices. Servant Leadership has inverted the antiquated organization chart where leaders support the employees.

Day care centers, laundry pickup and delivery, workout centers, and meditation rooms in the offices are just a few of the ideas fostered by entrepreneurial leaders. Free food, flexible work hours, working from home. And more.

> Enabling employees is at the front of entrepreneurial leadership. *"As we look ahead, leaders will be those who empower others."*
>
> – Bill Gates

The bottom lines

A burning idea. The spark of new products, businesses, and industries. Entrepreneurial leaders are passionate, focused, planners, cash-smart, employee centered, customer conscious, and bulldog persistent. And they invent new leadership models to support success. Be an entrepreneurial leader. Even in an existing company.

LEADERSHIP LESSON 8

SUCCESSFUL LEADERSHIP: ALIGNING PLANS, PEOPLE, AND ASSETS

Luck? The alignment of the planets? They do not support the sustainable success of a good business. Leadership alone? Still not enough. But the combination of a legacy leader and their focus on the optimum alignment of their plans, people, and assets significantly increases the possibility of success. Short and long term.

The strategic business plan of a company outlines important things: purpose, vision, mission, values, goals, strategy, and actions. The key asset required to implement the plan is organized employees. Some other assets required include capital, facilities, products, markets, customers, vendors.

When the plan, the people, and the assets are not well aligned, trouble. And waste.

Wobbly wheels
Imagine that the business is a bus loaded with the plan (roadmap), the people (passengers), and the assets (gas, luggage). The

leader (driver) decides that it is time to drive toward the horizon of success.

The bus starts rocking, weaving side-to-side, passengers fall out of their seats, the driver drops the map, gas is spilling out, and luggage flies out the windows.

The steering is out of alignment and the bus is failing. Time for repairs.

At the start
Alignment is critical to all businesses and nonprofits. It is a conscious effort by great leaders to make certain that all parts of the organization play together. In good times and (especially) bad. Here are seven key elements of alignment:

1. Communicate the strategic business plan to every employee. It is the first step in knowing what to do.
2. Build a good company culture and invite the entire organization to live it in thoughts, words, and actions. Hire new employees that fit the culture.
3. Organize people so that their core strengths are amplified. Help them "do what they love, and love what they do."
4. Clarify functional rolls and responsibilities. Each individual and team needs to know what they are doing and for what reason.
5. Establish lines of communication so that every department is in touch with all other departments. Facilitate the free flow of information for everyone.
6. Mutually align with the "outside world" as much as possible. Include vendors, shareholders, the surrounding community.

7. Inspire performance to underwrite the value of alignment. Let everyone know that good things are happening because the business is aligned.

Legacy leaders practice alignment as a continuous process. Yet research suggests that over 50% of leaders have had little if any education about alignment and do not clearly know what "creating alignment" means. Time to start learning.

The aligned and the unaligned

Some enticing benefits of aligned businesses and organizations include: better use of resources; minimized personal agendas; increased focus; more productivity; improved creativity; and more.

Southwest Airlines has been a highly aligned organization from the beginning and a sustained business success. But Northwest Airlines was so poorly aligned that they suffered with bad morale and ultimate bankruptcy.

> *"It's stunning to me what kind of an impact even one person can have if they have the right passion, perspective and are able to align the interest of a great team."*
>
> – STEVE CASE, FOUNDER OF AOL.

The bottom lines

Plan. Then align everyone. And everything. Make on-going alignment a high priority responsibility of good leadership. Plan, organize, communicate, clarify, and get the organization moving together in the same direction. Sustainable success.

LEADERSHIP LESSON 9

COMPANY CULTURE, LEGACY LEADERS, AND SUSTAINABLE SUCCESS

Elusive. Company culture is a challenge to define, create, and build into an effective organization. And if leaders do not incubate, cultivate, and grow a good working culture, the organization will grow one of its own. And it might not be a good one. Creating culture is a core responsibility of legacy leaders. Culture counts.

It takes time, patience, and good leadership to infuse a positive culture. But the payoff is a great place to work and sustainable business success.

"Culture drives great results."

JACK WELCH, FORMER CEO OF GENERAL ELECTRIC.

What is it?
Culture is born out of values and behaviors held by leaders of the company. It forms the fabric of woven out of the combined beliefs and principles held by members of the organization itself.

It includes many elements such as vision, mission, history, strategy, products, systems, habits, assumptions, symbols, and more.

Culture is the foundation of how employees think, communicate and act with others – inside and outside the organization. Collective psychology in action. A way of business life.

Cultivating culture

Good leaders build a strong culture out of their positive values and by their demonstrated actions. If the leader is authentic, an open communicator, focused, team player, and driven to excellence – the organization will behave similarly.

If a positive culture is already established, then the leader can preserve and amplify it. The tougher task is to move a negative tradition up to higher ground. It takes time and the constant demonstration by a good leader to make a positive shift. Launching, communicating, and enacting new values is a good staring point. Conversely, force-feeding a new culture into an organization often backfires. Badly.

Some tips for developing and changing culture include: clarify and communicate the purpose (the "why") of the organization; hire people who fit the desired culture; appoint someone to be the culture champion; empower and trust people; provide a positive workplace.

Positive proof

Here are three examples of outstanding company cultures based upon surveys reported in *Business Insider:*

> Southwest Airlines has long been known as a great place to work. Its culture emphasizes empathy for its employees, a happy place to work, and helpfulness to each other and customers. The company has been consistently profitable for decades. "The people are friendly and helpful. The culture fosters hard work and fun."
>
> – SOUTHWEST AIRLINE ANALYST.

Facebook's headquarters was inspired by Disneyland, but the goodies are free.

> "Huge impact on billions of people while working with awesome, insanely intelligent coworkers at a pleasant office. Great free food and perks. Lots of autonomy and big problems to solve."
>
> – FACEBOOK SOFTWARE ENGINEER.

> Edelman, a public relations firm, is one of the top 50 employers people want to work for, per LinkedIn. "Through the actions of middle to senior management, you are truly made to feel valued and appreciated. Opportunities are everywhere and the culture is laid back and fun."
>
> – EDELMAN SENIOR VICE PRESIDENT.

The culture of an organization is the root of its success. Or failure.

The bottom lines
Get culture. Build, upgrade, sustain a positive organizational culture. It is the lifeblood of company growth and sustainable success. Find out what it is and take time to improve and protect it. Base it upon the purpose and values of the company. As a leader, live your culture. Daily.

LEADERSHIP LESSON 10

THE FIVE PILLARS OF LEADERSHIP FOR SUCCESSFUL PROJECTS

The project died. Who messed up? The leader. A University of Ottawa study notes that 33% of projects fail for lack of involvement by a senior leader. The Project Management Institute indicates that 67% of all projects fail to meet their goals. Why risk it?

Even if a project is still alive, it might be ill: behind schedule, several key elements missing, way over budget, filled with errors, unnecessary features have been added, no documentation. A mess in the making.

What to do? Leaders must implement the 5 pillars of project success: Plan, People, Process, Polish-off, Post-completion.

Plan

"Planning is everything." Call it requirements, scope, boundaries, definition, intent. Get a team together to lay out and document all aspects of the project: expected outcomes, deliverable items, milestones, priorities, target costs, budget. The more detailed the plan, the smoother the project will go. Everything.

People

"Who's in charge?" Not just key managers, but who is the executive leader who is committed to be involved and drive the project to success? Who is on the team? How is the team structured? What functional organizations are involved? Define roles and responsibilities. Document and communicate. Everybody.

Process

"Many moving parts." How will the project will be managed? What are the lines of communication, frequency of meetings to report progress and isolate issues, risks, reports, checklists, testing, and audits? Record the process, communicate it, update it when necessary, fix it when it is broken. Every time.

Polish-off

"It ain't over till it's over." How will the leader, team, and others know that everything is done? Given the Plan, the People, and the Process, the team needs to collectively determine that everything called for is complete. All the deliverables are delivered and the recipients agree. Every checklist is checked. Hold a team meeting to ask the question, "What is missing?" When everything is complete, get all the signoffs needed. Then it's party time to celebrate success and recognize heroes. Everywhere.

Post-completion

"How can we do better next time?" There is always something to learn from a good debriefing. Let everyone share into a document that describes what worked well, what didn't work so well, and why. What could have been done differently and what should be changed next time? Publish the resulting record so that all can learn and benefit. Everyway.

Helpful hints

Here are some things that professional project managers have learned:

- Pad the milestone dates to allow for unforeseen slippages.
- Make timely decisions or the project will slow down.
- Make it safe for everyone to speak up for more knowledge and clarity.
- Simplify everything possible and eliminate redundancies to save time.
- Use good project management software tools for more efficiency.

And anytime there is "scope creep" (unplanned things being added), approve or kill it.

Bad news, good news

In 2006 the Airbus 380 jumbo jet was two years late and overran budget by $6 billion due to poor project management.

In 1969 the United States voyage to the moon was a stellar example of extraordinary project management – a massive, high-risk project completed on time.

The bottom lines
Personal involvement. Good leaders do it with key projects. They implement and track 5 pillars of project management: Plan, People, Process, Polish-off, Post-completion. Lower risk, lower cost, on-time. Successful projects and organizations. And people.

LEADERSHIP LESSON 11

ADVANCED MARKETING: WHO IS THE CUSTOMER OF YOUR CUSTOMER?

What? Why should we be interested in who is impacted by our customers' purchases? It is enough of a challenge to find and serve markets for our own customers. The answer can improve our own business. If we know what motivates our buyers to serve their markets, we can help both our customers and their customers. Call it a win-win-win.

SONR Labs was providing internal hardware and software to the manufacturer of a docking station for smart phones to play music. SONR got an idea from a customer of the dock provider. Add the capability to also use the dock as a speaker phone.

New idea from a customer of our customer. More business for both SONR and its customer. Synergy.

B2B
Business-to-business. When your business is providing products to other businesses, it is time to do deep research about your

customers – and their customers. What is their business plan: purpose, vision, mission/markets, values, goals, strategies, financial profile?

Why do your customers buy from you? And why do their customers buy from your customer? What do those end buyers do with their purchases? What else do the end customers want from your customer?

The more information you have about your buyers and those who buy from them, the more opportunity you have to serve both. Double decker.

B2C
Business-to-consumer. If your business is selling directly to the end consumer, then there is no need to go further, right? Not really. Your marketing should include not only where and who are your existing and potential consumers - you need to find out why your consumers are buying from you.

And, what are they doing with their purchases? Likely more than you think. Their "customers" might be their family, friends, nonprofits they serve, offices in which they work. Perhaps artistic avocations in which they sell the stuff of their creativity.

In finding out, you will do a better job of serving them – and those they serve.

How do you find out?
Treat your customers as a partner, not just as a customer. Don't "love 'em and leave 'em." Stay close to them in a number of ways:

Ask them – make direct inquiries about their business and let them know why. You are wanting to do a better job for them and their customers.

Share research – give your important customers the benefit of the research you to about them, their industry, and their customers. Help your customers and theirs.

Joint calls – if possible, make some calls with your customers to their customers. If you know what the end buyers want, you'll have a better opportunity to assist your customers.

Create ideas – generate new concepts for your customers to enhance their business with their present and potential buyers. And, ask them for ideas that will help you.

Co-brand – offer to extend your strong brand to help your customer's brand. "Intel Inside" is a classic example of how a big brand supported the branding of PC providers.

Go all out to serve your customers to better serve theirs. You win and so do they.

The bottom lines

Go wide. Market deeply. Don't just serve your customers. Help them serve their customers. Find out everything you can about both. Build business for customers, their customers, and you. Both B2B and B2C. Win-win-win.

LEADERSHIP LESSON 12

HERE'S HOW LEADERS SET BOUNDARIES FOR OTHERS (AND THEMSELVES)

Rules. Guidelines. Barriers. From the time we were children we did not care for them. Until we later found out their necessity. In school and at work. Not passing a course was debilitating. Failure in a job was career threatening. But observing the rules could bring graduation and job promotions. Success.

Good leaders often create rules and guidelines to protect good employees, customers, vendors, the organization, and the business.

Above all, well-constructed rules and guidelines facilitate good work well done for the organization and its people. Smooth operations.

Rewards and penalties

Leaders incent employees for following guidelines, rules, and barriers. Rewards for good behavior and performance are far more appealing to most people than punishment for breaking rules and ignoring guidelines. Such as losing a job.

Barriers have two aspects: normally we must not breach the "do not cross the line" warnings. The opposite case is when we are asked to move through a barrier to succeed with challenging projects.

It is important to let the organization know what is expected of everyone, what the potential rewards are, and the consequences for breaking the rules. Clarity counts.

How to build a boundary

Learn how to construct, manage, and enforce boundaries. Rules are usually rigid, and guidelines are typically more flexible. Define which is which and what you mean by each. Here are some tips for constructing meaningful rules and guidelines:

<u>Value-based</u> – build rules and guidelines around the values of the organization so that they are congruous. And better understood.

<u>Leadership role</u> – you have the right to establish the principles by which the company is operated. You will be respected.

<u>Decisiveness</u> – establish clear rules, guidelines, and barriers and note that you expect them to be followed. The organization wants to know.

<u>Communication</u> – make certain that all guidelines and rules are communicated and posted to the entire organization. Tell new employees, too.

No one should have to guess at the rules. And when they change, communicate again.

Rules for self
As a true leader of your organization you need to form and follow some rules for your own self-care. Your own rulebook protects you, your family and friends, and your company. Be efficient, feel better, tolerate some stress. Avoid burnout.

Areas to focus on include: how much time you spend at your job – in the office, at home, and elsewhere; maintain a good diet; get enough sleep; exercise regularly, take some time off.

And learn to say no. "No is a complete sentence."

– ANNE LAMOTT

Both sides of the boundary
Well constructed rules, guidelines, and barriers help keep good employees in the organization. They know exactly what is expected of them – and the rewards and penalties for their behavior.

Similarly, good disciplines help keep unwanted people, products, and processes out of the company. Don't hire people that cannot measure up. Avoid vendors that do not meet your requirements. Stop processes that are not documented, taught, and followed.

"Start with good people, lay out the rules, communicate with your employees, motivate them and reward them."

– LEE IACOCCA

The bottom lines

Build boundaries. For your organization and for you. Base them on your values, assert your leadership role, be decisive, and communicate the rules and guidelines. Be consistent. Make and manage the fences of good leadership. For everyone's success.

LEADERSHIP LESSON 13

PERSISTENCE AND LEADERSHIP: BUSTING THROUGH BARRIERS TO SUCCESS

Don't quit. Especially when you are in the muddy slog of change and challenge. The long lists of strong leadership qualities often focus on integrity, communications, and positivity. And many more, including creativity, flexibility and vision. But persistence?

> "Nothing in this world can take the place of persistence. Talent will not: nothing is more common than unsuccessful men with talent. Genius will not; unrewarded genius is almost a proverb. Education will not: the world is full of educated derelicts. Persistence and determination alone are omnipotent."
>
> – Calvin Coolidge

Ask any successful entrepreneur about persistence. They are experts.

The great inner barriers
Don't believe that factors outside ourselves are the only big brick walls we face. The larger and thicker barricades are inside us. They include:

Self-criticism – the whirring hum of our inner voice that says, "You can't do this; you are too young (or old); you lack knowledge; you are inexperienced." Muzzle this mouth.

Creeping doubt – disbelief in ourselves; we have taken on too much; competition will kill this; we will never get enough capital; this will never work. Buck up and believe.

Naysaying bystanders – do not internalize those who say, "You are out of your mind; think about the organization; this will fail; you are wasting time." Ignore them.

Negative emotions – commonly enough, a full buffet of emotional garbage shows up as despair, guilt, resentments, irritation, anxiety, and more. Flush them.

Burnout bruises – long hours and many days of persevering against organizational and personal challenges can slow and stop leaders and others. Rest, then persevere.

Learn that all the above barriers can beat down all but the strongest. Protect yourself from yourself.

Outer obstacles

Sure. There are all the ongoing situations that strong leaders must face and resolve in some way. Limited staffing, lack of capital, strong competitors, shifting markets, organizational disruptions, rising costs, a failed product, government policies. Endless.

The leaders who overcome these normal roadblocks have learned from business gurus, Peter Drucker, to "Do the right things right," and Steven Covey to "Do the first things first." They are excellent priority setters, expert time managers, and effective decision makers.

Strong leaders set goals, anticipate risks, demonstrate fast flexibility, build and sustain supportive teams, foster innovation and change, stay positive, and celebrate success. Repeatedly.

They did it!

History is packed with stories of success for those who persevered. Good examples include:

Thomas Edison overcame a childhood hearing impairment before running 10,000 experiments to develop the electric light bulb. He formed a dozen companies, including General Electric. Edison invented the microphone, phonograph, and motion pictures. His persistence changed the world for good.

Henry Ford had three automotive startup failures before launching the Ford Motor Company. He developed the first assembly lines and overpaid his employees. Ford's globally successful corporation persists today and we are the benefactors.

Winston Churchill was England's spark plug to survive and thrive in WWII and beyond. His indelible quote is, "Never, never, never give up." A mantra for persistence.

Do not "throw in the towel" – wash it, dry it, and use it again tomorrow.

The bottom lines
Don't quit. Especially what we believe in. Monitor and manage negative thoughts. Overcome external barriers to progress with great leadership. Prioritize and do the right things right. Learn from leaders who perfected persistence. Never give up.

LEADERSHIP LESSON 14

HOW NIMBLE LEADERS CURE SICK BUSINESSES: A FIVE-STEP TURNAROUND

Ouch! The pain of a crippled or dying business is unbearable. It is time for a turnaround before it is too late. Don't give up on the patient. There are known steps to take. While there are no guarantees, good actions can revive a good business. Quickly.

Call an ambulance and do not hide the problem (likelihood is that others in the organization already know). Put the business and organization on the examination table and engage your best ER team.

Take five steps: triage, diagnosis, surgery, recovery, prevention. Oh, and celebrate success.

1. Triage
Stop the bleeding. Find the greatest damage in the organization and apply a tourniquet. Where are the largest cash wounds? Reduce those costs as quickly as possible. And other related costs if necessary.

When appropriate, let the family of employees, vendors, customers, and other stakeholders know what is happening. Invite their support and participation. Honesty matters.

2. Diagnosis

What are the real unseen causes of the ills? Is it constricted development of new products and services? How about constipated marketing? A blockage in new sales? Does customer service have a neural breakdown. Is there a toxic culture?

Worse, does the organization have blurred vision, purpose, values, mission, goals, and strategies? Head to the operating room and get scrubbed up. Now.

3. Surgery

Assemble your team and decide how to proceed. If you need outside expertise, get it. Here are some learned inputs about turnaround operating procedures.

Communicate the plan. The organization wants to know the turnaround plan and that someone competent is leading the company ably forward. Communicate progress, too.

Care for employees. Make certain they are honestly informed about what is happening and what is being done about it. Enlist their support. Pay them fully and on time.

Manage all cash. Now is the time for the CFO to shut down all unnecessary cash expenditures. And search for possible added capital.

Reduce headcount bloat. Start with management. People are the most important asset, but evaluate them honestly. Do it swiftly and humanely to preserve morale.

Make team-based decisions. Use trusted staff members and outside experts. Move quickly on every decision.

Don't cut marketing. Drive more revenues and profitability by spending well for amplified marketing and sales. Update marketing plans with opportunities for growth.

Revisit business plans. Do the company's vision, values, mission, goals, strategies, and actions still make sense? If not, revamp and communicate them with clarity.

Given the possibility of a successful rebuild, give the business time to heal.

4. Recovery
There may be lingering pain in the organization. Friends were laid off, change is stressful, and ultimate success is a question. But by working smart and supporting each other quickly, recovery will likely progress. "Time heals all wounds."

5. Prevention
Prevent recurrence. Operate the business as if it is a turnaround all of the time. Why not?

They turned around
A recent article in *Fortune Magazine*, "Best Buy and four other blockbuster corporate turnarounds," conveys the stunning

successes of Apple, Ford Motor, Xerox, Starbucks, plus Best Buy. http://fortune.com/2015/03/04/best-buy-turnaround-stories/

The bottom lines

Pain. The business is sick and the organization is contaminated. It is time to heal the company. Fast. Follow the five steps to healing and good business health: triage, diagnosis, surgery, recovery, and prevention of recurrence. Be well.

LEADERSHIP LESSON 15

SOUL OF THE LEADER: ESSENCE OF THE ORGANIZATION

It's a spiritual thing. The invisible inner-being of legacy leaders becomes visible in taking action. Soul. Call it spirit, essence, or source. It is the vital force behind our thoughts, words, and actions. Leaders understand it and tap into this "inner voice" to manifest their vision, values, mission, strategies, and actions. Listen to it.

Our inner voice calls us, nudges, or sometimes shoves us – into increasing levels of greatness. Particularly when we can focus on service to others: employees, customers, vendors, communities, and other stakeholders.

Leaders know that their soul-being becomes the essence of their organization. Purpose.

Self-leadership first

Constant self-mastery and development become the foundation of great leaders. If we cannot lead ourselves, we will not lead others. The top three qualities of standout leaders are integrity, communication, and positivity.

Integrity is the stem for ethics, trust, and always doing the right thing. Communication is two-way, in-person, phone, email, text, or videoconference – and good listening is paramount. Positivity attracts other upbeat and talented people, retains them, and releases the best in them.

Above all, authenticity is a visible outpouring of the soul of the leader. It infuses and ignites organizations that work miracles. Always.

Soul-purpose in action
As the soul-purpose emerges from the inner-being of the leader, it morphs into the vision, values, mission, strategy, and action that propels a successful organization.

Ultimate action. If there is no action, there is no leader:

- Purpose – why does the organization exist, what does it do for our world, what grand cause does it stand for. It is the motivating force and a constant compass. The purpose of McGraw-Hill Companies is "creating economic growth, job creation, and a smarter, better world."
- Vision – how the organization will look to the outside world and internally in the coming years, including the benefits provided to employees, customers and others.
- Values – describe the top essential beliefs and behaviors through which the organization conducts itself. These values define the character of the organization.

- Mission – what the business does for whom and why. The primary products and services the organization provides. The broad scope of the business.
- Strategy – the goals and the overarching direction of the business in recognition of a competitive market. Strategy guides right choices in allocating limited resources.
- Actions – the critical activities by the organization to achieve the critical goals. Ergo, what to do, when, where, and by whom. Actions assigned to specific responsible and accountable people. Progress is measured frequently.

This is the path that transforms the soul of legacy leaders into the soul of their legacy organizations.

Potholes in the path

Most great leaders have overcome great personal and professional obstacles to become greater leaders. Often, they have needed to discern the "other voice" of their ego and shut it off.

As a young lawyer, Gandhi's anger almost destroyed him. He reflected, drew calmness from his inner strength, and led a nation to freedom through non-violence.

> *"Nothing splendid has ever been achieved except by those who dare believe that something inside of them was superior to circumstance."*
>
> – AUTHOR BRUCE BARTON

The bottom lines

Listen. Pay attention to the voice of your inner-being. Understand your purpose. Transform the organization from your spirit of vision, values, mission, strategy, and action. Avoid the disruptive voice of ego. Follow your soul. Essence.

LEADERSHIP LESSON 16

THIS IS WHY GREAT LEADERS CHOOSE GREAT CFO'S

Bean counter? No longer. The Chief Financial Officer, regardless of actual title, is the best friend of the CEO and other organizational leaders. The CFO can make or break a business. Far more than accounting statements and financial activities, the right CFO mitigates critical risks and is a strategic thinker. Always.

The growing sophistication of finance and accounting regulations and reports, increased interaction with outside organizations, tax requirements, oscillating market forces, and the sheer velocity of business demand a good CFO.

Outside investors, boards of directors, and publicly traded companies all drive elevated business complexity. Entanglement ensues.

CFO saves Pandora from drowning

Listen to this. In 2013 Internet radio company Pandora was struggling with profitability. The CEO hired a new CFO, Michael Herring. One month later the CEO unexpectedly resigned.

Herring's predecessors argued with musicians to lower their royalties. Herring saw this as a mistake. Instead, he made a strategic decision to limit the number of free listeners. Advertising demand was climbing. So, ad pricing and revenues rose. Herring did strategic deals with ad agencies, attracted competitors' listeners, and once again allowed unlimited free listening. Profitability soared.

Pandora hired a new CEO who saw Michael Herring's greatness as a strategic CFO. Herring continues as the CFO. A hero.

Great CFO's defined

If you could build an outstanding CFO, what would the parts look like? Here is a proven shopping list:

<u>Ethical</u> – untainted integrity, trusted by every constituent, custodian of all matters money, always willing to let the CEO know about bad news (no matter what).

<u>Confident</u> – solid in facts and beliefs, not prideful, maintains the trust of everyone even in challenging circumstances.

<u>Knowledgeable</u> – well versed and experienced in accounting and finance, excellent cash management skills, uses qualified outside experts as needed.

<u>Creative</u> – knows the organization, recognizes and solves problems skillfully, uses resources to plan ahead, works well with people, isn't just about numbers.

Reliable – handles pressure to provide on-time reports and results, fosters appropriate change, instigates new methods for efficiency.

Understanding – comprehends the full extent of business functions and operations, accurately and quickly interprets situations.

Productive – works diligently for the good of all, high output including the details, admits mistakes and corrects them quickly, works as many hours as it takes.

Communicative – especially in high-pressure situations, delivers written and spoken reports to key people, anticipatory, a receptive listener.

Strategic – helps set the overall direction of the business, a leader within the organization, assists with business models and plans, great negotiator.

Effective – results oriented, does not let process or problems stop progress, a team builder and motivator.

The best CFO is the CEO's best friend.

Superhuman

If the above list is not enough, here are some additional qualities of excellent CFO's and other financial leaders: mentors and coaches others; decisive; works with others for mergers and acquisitions, legal, employee benefits, financing, IT, insurance;

establishes and measures key metrics of performance; works well with boards and investors; seeks opportunity in complex and ambiguous situations; insightful.

The bottom lines

Count on them. Every organization needs a chief financial officer by any title. The one who unwaveringly cares for the overall monetary welfare of everyone involved. Honest, open, skilled, strategic, team player, not just about numbers. Does what it takes for everyone to win. Best friend of the CEO. For good.

LEADERSHIP LESSON 17

LEADERSHIP AND THE GREAT COMPUTER BURIAL GROUND

"IT". Information Technology can take on a life of its own. When the technology is more important than the information, something is missing. The customers are not served, employees are less productive, vendors are confused, and the accountants are in rebellion. What's wrong? Don't blame "IT" – look at leaders.

Today entire corporations and smaller organizations run completely dependent upon computers. Take away IT and there is no business.

The greater issue is not when IT is down (usually a short period of time). It is when IT is ineffective (typically a long period of time). Time for leadership.

Software vs. brainware

Too many assumptions about IT are made by too many leaders, including:

1. The IT department holds the best interests of customers, employees, others.
2. A CIO knows everything there is to know about hardware, software, systems.
3. Computer vendors are completely altruistic and always provide the best.
4. All IT systems produced for the organization are easy to use.
5. Training and support is thought out from the beginning.
6. Room for future changes is designed into the system.
7. Nothing ever becomes obsolete and the company's business will not change.
8. Just because the system design works on paper, it will work in fact.
9. Hardware and software vendors never go out of business.
10. The IT system is smarter than the humans who use it.

Good leaders challenge all the above and more. All the time. Sensibility.

A big botch

Knight Capital Group enjoyed an excellent reputation as a market-maker company. Until August 2012, that is. On the morning of August 1 some of its computer software trading formulas got a bug. Instead of "buy low, sell high" the system did the opposite. It flipped into a "buy high, sell low" strategy for over 100 stocks. The loss was a near-instant $440 million. The stock price dropped over 60% in a single day. Four months later the company agreed to be acquired. Control-alt-delete.

IT to-do list

Turn the complex into the common by following three, simple suggestions:

Prevention – begin with people. Hire the best CIO (chief information officer) or IT manager. Enforce the hiring of top-grade IT people. Systems designers, programmers, testers, documenters, support. Give them the best tools and facilities they need. Hire fewer people, hire better people.

Process – insist upon regular meetings to make progress with new systems and the performance of existing systems. Ask people to stand up and report their areas of responsibility. Isolate and resolve issues as a team. Openly reward the heroes.

Payment – most IT projects exceed budget. There is overkill in many areas because the developers want to make it "cool" (scope creep). A good reason to demand accurate, documented design and development documents. Don't throw out old gear. Use it on simpler projects. Or sell it.

If the organization must have great IT, great leaders must participate. Enter.

> "All sorts of computer errors are now turning up. You'd be surprised to know the number of doctors who claim they are treating pregnant men."
>
> – Isaac Asimov

The bottom lines
Get IT. But make no assumptions. Hire the best IT people and give them the best tools. Prevent problems, use processes to make progress, and carefully manage IT budgets. Be involved. Control IT before IT controls you. Click.

LEADERSHIP LESSON 18

WHY "NO STRINGS ATTACHED" LEADERSHIP SUCCEEDS

Unknot. Organizations play follow-the-leader. When leaders are entangled in inappropriate webs of external or internal power, parts or all of an organization can suffer, decline, or fail. But when a leader is not tied unduly to someone else's influences, pressures, or demands, that leader is free to lead in more honest and authentic ways. Businesses, nonprofits, governments.

Enron Corporation's leadership was over-influenced by the White House staff, J P Morgan Chase, Arthur Anderson, and a lair of lobbyists. In the 2001 crash landing of the company, an entire organization of several thousand people was destroyed. Shareholder's stakes went from $90 to $0 within a few weeks.

Some people went to prison. People who had strings attached to them.

Influences, pressures, demands
Enron was an extreme case of inappropriately being influenced and being the influencer. But what about small and midsize organizations? The symptoms are similar, if not the same. Leaders who succumb to undue influence, inordinate pressure, and unreasonable demands weaken their organization.

Consider the possible sources of unfitting manipulations of organizational leaders: board members, individual shareholders, large vendors, key employees, government, lobbyists, top executives, and unions. Overbearing customers, too.

There is a potential Enron lurking in organizations whose leaders have a string attached. Or a rope around their neck.

Red flags
Here are some warning signs of leaders who have some strings of influence attached to them:

- Wavering – their decisions and actions are not grounded, rapid or durable.
- Distant – they withdraw, become less approachable, and seem secretive.
- Stagnant – their normal creative, innovative approaches decline.
- Slower – the pace of activity dampens in most or all of the organization.
- Muted – communications are slow, with less information, less frequent.
- Alone – teamwork suffers, inputs are not solicited, and feedback is not given.

- Autocratic – a once-democratic leader becomes more dictatorial.

Overall, the situation tends to get worse. Unless the leader snips the strings.

Leaders unleashed

Courageous leaders will not only recognize the inappropriate pressures being placed upon them, but they will do something about it. They will face up to the purveyors of pressure, hold authentic conversations with them, and ask for a change.

Authentic leaders have the best in mind for their organizations, their employees, customers, vendors, communities, boards, shareholders, and others. They do not succumb to threats, however veiled. They hold the high watch for the greater good of all.

When all else fails, the outstanding leader would rather give up their job than be a puppet to unreasonable power. They do not play for politics. They play for people.

About face

The reverse is true, too. Authentic leaders do not attach strings to others. They are honest, open, transparent, and forthright in their relationships with everyone. They attract the same kinds of people to them. People who give themselves to the best possible outcomes of their organization and everyone involved.

These leaders avoid the inappropriate influences, pressures, and demands of others. They draw their real power from within, not from others.

> *"The minute you succumb to outside pressure, you cease to be creative."*
>
> – Vilayanur S. Ramachandran

The bottom lines

Untangle. No-strings-attached. Refuse inappropriate, strings-attached influences, pressures, and demands. Don't ignore them – get rid of them and be authentic. And do not attach strings to your people. Perform as an honest leader and your organization will follow you. Trust your own power. Always.

LEADERSHIP LESSON 19

FIND OUT HOW LEADERS HANDLE CONFLICTS EFFECTIVELY

Disagree. We do not always see eye to eye. It happens in every organization. A question is, "to what degree?" Most minor squabbles are self-correcting or resolved quickly. Big battles can destroy entire businesses. Those are the ones that need to be stopped. Good leaders smell the fumes of organizational brush fires and race to squelch them. Quickly.

Symptoms? Dissension about new product features. Friction over who owns responsibility for a process. A clash regarding a sales territory. Incompatibility with a key staff member.

The results can be time consuming, morale busting, and financially costly.

Where is the smoke?
Leaders in the know utilize several strategies to quell harmful conflicts. But first it is critical to really understand the nature of the discord. Some questions will help pull the pieces apart:

Who is involved, why has the disagreement formed, what is at stake, where in the organization (and outside of it) are the effects of the conflict, and when is it showing up?

Once these and other questions are understood, it is time to get all the opposing people together. Then get everyone's inputs and opinions. And especially their suggestions for resolving the dissension. Fairly.

A, B, C, D, E resolution strategies

Depending upon the makeup of the conflict, here are five A to E approaches that strong leaders utilize to dissolve an issue:

- Adjudication – the leader hears all arguments from both sides, makes a learned judgment, and decides for one side or the other.
- Balance – work a series of give and takes with both sides until an acceptable, perhaps not completely agreeable, solution is derived.
- Collaboration – bring ideas together to formulate a creative solution that will be acceptable to all (or as many as possible).
- Delay – choose not to force an immediate decision, give the process some additional measured time, see if the problem is self-resolving, and revisit the issue later.
- Elimination – throw out ideas that do not appeal to either side, get rid of the past and focus on the future, ditch blame and look for positive solutions.

In the end, strong leaders negotiate the best solutions. Smoothly.

Conflict resolution tools

While working the A, B, C, D, and E strategies noted above, there are some additional common sense means of dissolving disagreements in business organizations of all kinds and sizes.

Among them are always staying positive, looking for innovative solutions, asking constructive questions, restating conversations for clarity, listening for meaning, focusing on the problem (not on personalities), connecting like thoughts, amplifying similarities and downplaying differences.

> *"Peace is not absence of conflict; it is the ability to handle conflict by peaceful means."*
>
> – RONALD REAGAN

Big financial sinkhole

In 2008 publisher CPP Inc., publishers of the Meyers-Briggs and Thomas-Kilmann Conflict Mode instruments, did a study on workplace conflict. One finding in the United States was that employees spent an average 2.8 hours per week managing conflict. That amounted to nearly $360 billion in paid wages; the equivalent of 385 million working days. Massive. Important enough to prompt efficient conflict identification and resolution. And prevention.

The bottom lines

Be alert. Sniff out any simmering or bonfire conflicts in your organization. Get the right players together, strategize a resolution, and use good conflict resolution tools in the process. Save money. Save time. Save the organization. Prevent future fires. No smoke.

LEADERSHIP LESSON 20

DO YOU HAVE IT IN YOU TO BE A REAL LEADER?

Find out. You might be surprised to learn the level of leadership qualities you have. Or not. Several articles in contemporary media call out the most important characteristics of successful leaders. *Forbes, Inc.,* and *Fortune* magazines periodically point out the top attributes of top leader. Consistently.

How many positive leadership characteristics are there? When the various lists are combined and similar qualities are eliminated, the resulting list is smaller. By finding the most frequently stated leadership attributes, the top ten are found.

And there is one overarching quality. Guess?

A clarification
Before peeking ahead, there is an important distinction to make. Leaders, managers, and their contrasts:

- Leaders lead people. Managers manage processes.
- Leaders create and communicate the vision. Managers follow the vision.

- Leaders take the first step. Managers take the next step.
- Leaders ask "why" and "what." Managers ask "how" and "when."
- Leaders align people. Managers organize people.
- Leaders motivate and inspire. Managers administrate and direct.
- Leaders mentor, teach, and demonstrate. Managers coach, tell, and push.
- Leaders challenge the status quo. Managers work with the status quo.
- Leaders unleash potential. Managers coordinate resources.

This does not mean at all that managers have lesser values than leaders. And, there are leaders at every level of an organization. Including individual employees. We need both leaders and managers.

Top ten characteristics
Here are the leading qualities of successful leaders throughout different industries and sizes of organizations:

1. *Integrity* – being honest, truthful, reliable, consistent, open, responsible, and accountable in all situations and conditions.
2. *Communicating* – fostering open two-way information flow with employees, customers, and others; speaking, writing, and (especially) listening.
3. *Affirmative* – being positive, bold, courageous, optimistic, with a bias toward decisive action.
4. *Mindfulness* – staying self-aware, respectful of others, intuitive, instinctual, anticipatory, and conscious of the work environment.

5. *Initiator* – innovating creative new streams of people, products, services, processes, markets, and actions to build sustainable success for the business.
6. *Supportive* – being trustworthy, building trust, committed, delegating, responsive, dedicated, and engaged, cooperative, and collaborative.
7. *Principled* – holding high values for self and organization, humble, ethical in all matters, treating everyone fairly, composed, calm, and empathetic.
8. *Visionary* – casting a future that engages others, passionate about it, strategic around the vision, and highly focused on it.
9. *Team builder* – engaging, connecting with people, natural networker, involved, recognizing and rewarding exceptional work, persuasive, clear about goals.

10. Authenticity

Above all, legacy leaders are real. Authenticity attracts and inspires like-minded people. We are being authentic when we think, speak, and act from our heart and soul – our true inner self. Our character exhibits honesty and openness. We are seen as trusting and trustworthy.

It takes some courage to be authentic in business because we become vulnerable when we allow our often-protected inner self to be visible. But the rewards of established soul-to-soul, heart-to-heart connections can be enormous.

Authenticity does not answer the question of, "Who am I?" Authenticity affirms who I am. Others get it.

The bottom lines
Are you a real leader? Test yourself. Look at the above 10 key qualities of great leaders and score yourself 1 to 10 points for each quality you have. Add up your points. Relax because even the best leaders do not reach 100. Enhance your leadership qualities constantly. Be a real leader.

LEADERSHIP LESSON 21

DISCOVER WHY "MINDFULNESS" IS KEY TO LEGACY LEADERSHIP

Fad? Not really. Just a long-known phenomenon with a new name. Over many years it has been called: consciousness, focus, self-awareness, concentration, relaxation. In the past it was seemingly the domain of eastern philosophy and for personal use. No longer. Now, mindfulness is in western full bloom, taught by universities, and flowing into the business world. Why?

One early nudge was the publicity given to meditation starting in the 1960's. Propelled by the Beatles in song and by writers such as Dr. Herbert Benson of Harvard University, meditation became an increasingly staple practice. And, it wound its way into businesses. Big businesses, such as Google. So, what's the connection between meditation and mindfulness?

Simple. Meditation promotes mindfulness.

Academia speaks

One academic definition of mindful awareness is that it pays attention to present moment experiences with openness, curiosity, and acceptance. It invites us to stop, breathe, observe, and connect with our inner experience.

One contemporary teacher of mindfulness who has gained acclaim is Dr. Jon Kabat-Zinn of the University of Massachusetts Medical School. While a significant focus of his research and teachings are on stress reduction and wellbeing, he has attracted the corporate world as well.

Another university participating in the education of mindfulness is the University of California at Los Angeles (UCLA). Their Mindful Awareness Research Center (MARC) teaches mindfulness in the classroom. And online.

Business acts

The list of companies who have introduced mindfulness to their employees is long. And getting longer. Here are a few:

- Apple
- Deutsche Bank
- Procter & Gamble
- Aetna
- Google
- General Mills

Financial Times notes that General Mills makes mindfulness part of their corporate culture. One stated result is that after a seven-week course, 83% of the learners reported that they had started a practice of taking time to plan and optimize their productivity – daily. Before the course only 23% reported doing this.

Google has been teaching meditation to its employees from the beginning of the company. Now it is one of the largest, profitable, and best companies to work for.

Leaders lean in
In the above case of General Mills 80% of the senior executives who participated noted that they make better decisions. And 89% became better listeners.

Guess who prompted meditation and mindfulness to be taught in corporations, small and midsize businesses, and non-profits? Their leaders.

Books abound. If you search for books about mindfulness and leadership, here are some contemporary examples: *The Mindful Leader; The Mindfulness Edge; Mindful Leadership; Finding the Space to Lead; Leadership and Mindful Behavior.*

More ...
Meditation and mindfulness is now taught on a large scale. And in a non-religious context. Yet, some teachers and students believe that there is a spiritual context for meditation. Most likely you will find many nearby sources to learn meditation. Easily.

Beyond stress reduction, the list of benefits attributed to mindfulness is long: enhanced creativity, more efficient problem solving, improved productivity, better teamwork, a sense of overall well-being, less anxiety and depression, better handling of challenges.

And evidence suggests that mindful leaders and their mindful organizations excel in a competitive business world.

The bottom lines
Be mindful. Learn how to meditate and practice mindfulness. As a leader, as an individual, as an organization. Become more creative, focused, productive, resilient. Help your organization compete, succeed, and excel. Be happier, too.

LEADERSHIP LESSON 22

HOW LEARNING LEADERS BUILD LEARNING ORGANIZATIONS

New info. It keeps expanding at an increasing rate. About everything: leadership, management, business; technologies; organizational improvement; facilities and production; innovation and creativity; engineering methods. The opportunity to learn more about everything is pervasive. And necessary.

Great leaders understand this. They are life-long learners. They seek a meaningful, incoming stream of useful information that helps them be better leaders. Utilizing a very broad collection of resources. Internal and external.

And, these leaders want the same for their employees. Their budgets for education and training are significant. Their vision includes investing in their employees – organizationally and individually. Long term.

Into the classroom
Researcher and author Peter Senge used a term, "The Learning Organization" to describe a company that enables learning for its

employees. These businesses transform themselves continuously to thrive in a competitive environment.

Often, when businesses expand they do not automatically become learning organizations. The opposite occurs – they stop learning and individuals become more rigid in their thinking and behaviors. Solutions become more short term.

To become more competitive, companies must learn faster and run leaner than their opponents. And to do so, the employees must be armed with ever-new knowledge in a trusting, team-based environment.

Big campus

A number of corporations have emphasized the value of education with significant internal functions:

Motorola – during its peak, the company had formed Motorola University to drive education about many areas, including leadership, technology, and its well known Six Sigma Quality program. At one time the faculty was 1,000 people.

General Electric – its Management Development Institute in Crotonville, NY, provides a stream of learning for managers, who both learn and teach broad business topics.

Toyota – University of Toyota not only educates employees about the design and production of automotive products, it teaches their franchised dealers as well.

Other successful companies with prominent educational organizations include McDonald's Hamburger University, a 130,000 square foot facility with 80,000 graduates; Microsoft, Johnson & Johnson, Apple, USA Today, Southwest Airlines, Intel, and Disney. Give them an "A."

Arguably, organizations that stopped learning and adapting flunked: Greyhound Bus, Woolworths, Kodak, Gulf Oil. Their grade is "F."

Small campus

Smaller organizations use an array of tools to provide ongoing education for their employees: funding to support employee education at universities (classroom and online); employees taking turns to teach each other in a formal setting. "On The Job Learning."

Some colleges offer courses inside the business (Maricopa County Community College District in Phoenix does this with their Corporate College); monthly book discussions, where employees read a selected book and then discuss it together in a facilitated forum; outside seminars.

And, external experts can be brought in to teach specific workshops.

Passing the test

The many benefits of learning leaders and their learning organizations include:

- Enhanced job satisfaction and morale; being more people oriented.
- Boosting innovation and competitiveness; better response to external events.

- Accelerating the rate of proficient change; learning to flex and turn quickly.
- Strengthening customer bonding; providing contemporary sales and service.
- Improving quality across the organization; increasing productivity.

> *"An investment in knowledge pays the best interest."*
>
> – BENJAMIN FRANKLIN

The bottom lines

Wise up. Turn knowledge into action. Provide education for yourself and your organization. Build more responsive, flexible, and competitive companies. Seek internal and external resources to teach business, technical, communications, and other skills. Be life-long learners. Be smart.

LEADERSHIP LESSON 23

WHY YOU NEED TO STAMP OUT "SCOPE CREEP"

Risk. It has many facets. One of them is subtle, but a potentially costly business disease. "Scope creep." Not laboratory slip, not a Halloween character. It is the unintended expansion of a project, program, organization, or entire business.

Remarkably, scope creep is a frequent aspect of innocent, natural human behavior. "If a little is good, more is better, and a lot is best." Costly.

You have done a good job of planning. The required people, timelines, and budgets are in place. Things are moving forward in good order. Everyone is pleased. Except someone. Who?

Will the innocent please rise?
The unexpected expansion of pre-defined projects, products, processes – even people can be triggered unwittingly by leaders, managers, individual or groups of employees, customers, vendors, and others.

Here are some examples of how scope creep can get started:

- A new product is being designed and an engineer decides that it would nice to add an extra feature; it adds cost, complexity, time, and has no market.
- A manager keeps adding more employees to their staff because of perceived work overload; there is no budget, and no absolute need.
- A vendor tacks on some additional "handling" costs or unnecessary option; no one checks to validate the vendor's claim.
- A leader determines that the company should enter one more country beyond the business plan scope; the cost of doing so is high and that market is weak.
- A customer claims that their order was to include a special feature not originally defined; someone in sales agrees, profit margin is squeezed, delivery delayed.

In any form, unplanned add-ons have a sneaky way of adding cost, time, or both.

Words of warning

When you first hear these kinds of phrases, dig deep into what they mean before deciding anything – and teach your teams to do the same:

"Just one more thing …"; "I'm sure we told you …"; " "But we need this too …"; "We just realized …"; "That is not what we expected …"; "Why didn't you … ; "Wait, where is the … "

And, like weight gain, once project bloat starts it tends to continue. Stop it now.

How to put your foot down
Three tenets to preventing scope creep reside in fundamental management:

Clarity
Define and document everything possible about customer orders, product functionality, customer service guidelines, vendor specifications, production processes. Include all costs, prices, timelines. Document all changes. Don't make decisions without complete clarity. And, this can be done quickly if the decision process is spelled out. No bureaucracy needed.

Communications
Major mistakes are made when information about people, projects, products, and processes is not freely communicated among everyone who needs to know. Don't rely on documentation only – hold frequent meetings (phone, video, face-to-face) to track everything, and keep costs and schedules on-track. And flag unapproved scope creep.

Commitment
Assign the responsibility and accountability for projects and processes to mangers who will move things forward skillfully. They will deal with all out-of-scope issues and bring them up quickly for decisions by the right deciders.

Legendary leader Harold S. Geneen said it well, *"Management must manage."*

The bottom lines
Expensive. Scope creep is potentially everywhere. Initiated innocently by anyone. Once it starts it expands. Invoke strong management with clarity, communications, and commitment to stamp out scope creep. Quickly.

LEADERSHIP LESSON 24

WHAT IS THE "WHY" OF YOUR LEADERSHIP?

Vision? Mission? Values? Perhaps these are the roots of your leadership. Or, perhaps a focus on customers, employees, or shareholders. Maybe it is a desire to excel and succeed, to compete and win, or to be a hero. But, there is a higher level of understanding. Call it purpose.

"Why" is a contextual question. The answer to it establishes the purpose of people, places, and things. It clarifies situation, conditions, and factors. The answer sets a meaningful platform for leaders.

> *"Two great days in our lives: the day we are born and the day we discover why."*
>
> – WILLIAM BARCLAY

Those who knew their "why"

Great leaders who understand their "why" are rooted in wanting to make a positive difference in their sphere of influence by adding value to the lives of people. Employees, customers, constituents, and other stakeholders.

When Thomas Watson formed IBM in 1915, he established his purposeful "why" in one word: Think. Creative thinking that produced a stream of products and services to empower people with extraordinary information management.

John F. Kennedy's "why" was to unite a nation out of its malaise. One step was his May 25, 1961 statement; "… This Nation should commit itself, before this decade is out, of landing a man on the moon and returning him safely to earth." Round trip completed on July 24, 1969. Proud, united nation.

Legacy leadership

In numerous examples, great leaders such as Watson and Kennedy left something behind them of value to their world. Great organizations, pride of success in exceptional endeavors, advanced technologies, and more.

If the "why" of great leaders is the root and trunk of their strength, what are the durable branches that define the character of their thoughts, words, and actions? They are authentic, have broad visions that engage others, attract and retain great talent, and they produce an ongoing stream of outstanding products and services.

Added attributes, qualities, and characteristics

The top attributes that define durable leadership are: above all, honesty – openness, trust and transparency; communications – consistent, clear, and continuous; positivity – with everyone in all situations.

Lists of great leader characteristics also include:

- *Empowerment* leadership by and supporting employees.
- *Delegation* of authority, responsibility, and accountability.
- *Confidence* in the face of many obstacles.
- *Conviction* and commitment to visions, missions, and values.
- *Creativity* and resourcefulness in all aspects of the business and organization.
- *Intuition* and anticipation in sensing next steps, trends, and areas of risks.
- *Inspiring* others by more than words; taking decisive, meaningful actions.
- *Respect* and empathy for others in consistent ways.
- *Consistency* of thoughts, words, and actions.
- *Flexibility* in making appropriate changes.
- *Wisdom*, knowledgeable, continuously seeking and learning new information.

We are not superhuman although good leaders have many of these added qualities: organization, visibility, receptivity, courage, both persistence and patience, excellence, teamwork, example setting, goals based, boldness, fearless decision making, strategic, humility.

> *"Leadership is about making others better as a result of your presence and making sure that impact lasts in your absence."*
>
> – SHERYL SANDBERG, COO OF FACEBOOK

The bottom lines
"Why?" What is the purpose, meaning, or context of your leadership? If the answer is something other than creating sustainable good for others, you are missing something important. Firm in your purpose, add authenticity, honesty, communications and positivity – and other good leader qualities. Be a legacy leader.

LEADERSHIP LESSON 25

YOU FORGOT WHAT?
THE CRUCIAL BUSINESS
OF FOLLOW-UP

Boring? Seems so because most of us do not take time to follow-up on significant action items. Why? We are too busy. We would rather work on exciting new things instead. And we rationalize that it will take care of itself.

So, your doctor has diagnosed you with a serious physical disease. You have been asked to do a follow-up visit for a deeper look at the problem to find a solution. It could be life threatening. You don't follow-up. Good luck.

Details count big. Remember the adage, *"For want of a nail, the war was lost."*

Leaders and managers do it

Chaos theory describes the "butterfly effect" in how one flap of a butterfly's wings alters the space around it – and might set off a chain reaction of events that disrupt a greater space. Like an entire organization or business.

When a list of important actions has been determined, good leaders and managers must insist that those actions be completed. And those responsible for the implementations should be accountable for doing so. How?

Follow-up. The respective leaders and managers continuously track progress and results. Daily, weekly, monthly – depending upon the impact of the actions.

Hello program and project management

Some organizations hire one or more people only to focus on making certain that critical actions are organized, prioritized, and managed successfully to completion. These employees often carry a title of Program Manager.

Program Managers reach across all parts of an organization to achieve their mission. And, large programs are broken down typically into a network of interrelated projects with respective Project Managers.

Programs and projects teams hold frequent intra- and interoperational meetings to track actions, remove obstacles, uncover opportunities, highlight risks, and report progress. They are incented to drive results. And they love doing it.

Results, results, results

Strong follow-up, whether done by leaders and managers themselves, or by formalized program and project managers, triggers significant benefits: important things don't "fall through the cracks"; positive results occur sooner; priorities get proofed; next steps are always in view; budgets are better managed; the scope of activities is kept in bounds (scope-creep is stopped); bad programs and projects are stopped sooner.

Teams in name become teams in reality; motivation is lifted; roles and responsibilities are clarified; inter- and intra- department communications become more fluid. Overall, big follow-up costs less than big mistakes.

And (drumroll) revenue and profits are enhanced.

Mission impossible

Follow-up was hypercritical in one of our greatest accomplishments – the United States first voyage to the moon. Program and project managers were at the core of that incredible feat. Remember their indelible voices on July 20, 1969? Breathtaking!

Some best follow-up practices:

- Best employees will follow-up on their own actions; no need to push them.
- Follow-up practices question, "what, when, who, and where?"
- Some use the Agile Method as an effective program/project management tool.
- There are many software tools than can help – "Google it."
- Good follow-up can be taught and incented.

Remember this: *"Fortune follows follow-up."*

The bottom lines

Don't forget. Follow-up. Collect lists of all important action items. Organize by priorities. Include who is responsible and accountable, when are items due, where will the work take place. Leaders and managers can track everything. Better yet, get good program and project managers to do it. Get results.

LEADERSHIP LESSON 26

PLAN B: HOW TO CUT RISKS WITH PARALLEL STRATEGIES

Single threaded thinking. It can raise havoc with many business issues. Particularly strategy, which is the primary path of success. A singular strategy, however constructed, is a risk. Especially in the high-speed shifts of our global business economy.

A strategic plan is only as good as the planning that went into it. And a simple "risk analysis" in the back pages of the plan is weak – if it is based upon a single strategic direction.

Instead of considering potential risks at the end of the plan, look at them up front.

Single-strategy failures

Look at the failures in many industries that likely occurred because of weak planning.

Kodak got blurry when it was too late to combat the onslaught of digital photography. The original American, United,

Northwest, and other airlines were permanently grounded when they failed to recognize the strategic strength of low-cost airlines. Digital Equipment, Data General, Prime, and other minicomputer companies stopped running when the personal computer juggernaut outran them.

But Howard Shultz, upon acquiring the original Starbucks store, instituted the parallel strategies of: introducing expresso and other variations of coffee; transforming the "coffee shop" into a community gathering place; and migrated store-front coffee places to in-store coffee bars within grocery stores, book stores, and other retail stores. Coffee in our homes, too.

Parallel questions
Do a deep risk analysis at the start of every strategic business plan. And, good questions are the keys to unlocking the closet of risks:

- Who else is in this business and what percent of the market do they have?
- What are the three most compelling reasons someone will buy this product?
- Who will buy this product and why?
- Is there enough market demand to make it worthwhile being in this business?
- How much capital will be needed to launch this business, product, or service?
- Who will be the most likely competitors and why?
- What are the follow-on products now in planning that will sustain the business?

- How many employees will be needed and when, what are their skill sets, and will they be available in the necessary geographies?
- Are there any potential problems obtaining enough of the right kinds of materials?

More ...

- Are there any single-source vendors that could stop our plan?
- Is there a single part that would prevent our product from being provided?
- Are there any potential legal, compliance, or environmental issues in the way?
- What are the geographic considerations?
- Can we be one of the top three industry leaders?
- What if a competitor acquires another company to take market share?
- Does someone else hold any intellectual property, patents, trademarks, or rights that could be in the way?
- What would prevent the business from scaling up and then riding a cost curve down?

Summarize: what are the three to five worst things that could happen?

Plan B, C, D ...

Given the answers to the above and other questions, isolate the top risks. Then, form three to five parallel strategies that will eliminate or mitigate the risks. Build them into your strategic plan from the get-go.

The bottom lines
Start planning. Ask questions and trap the top risks to the business. Instead of one "Plan A" strategy, create multiple parallel strategies. Build the remainder of your strategic business plan around them. Crush risks. Enhance success.

LEADERSHIP LESSON 27

WHEN SHOULD GOOD LEADERS DEMAND GOOD DUE DILIGENCE?

Always. Due diligence is not something to do only when reviewing contracts. Or only when hiring a new employee, acquiring another company, or selecting a different vendor. Due diligence is an attitude of digging into details to make better decisions about important things. Remember the adage, "The devil is in the details?"

The deal devil

In 2000 America Online (AOL) of "you've got mail" fame acquired Time Warner for $165 billion. AOL had 25 million subscribers and a market capitalization of $175 million. But contrasting small revenues of $5 billion.

Time Warner's market capitalization was much less at $90 billion, but much larger revenues at $27 billion.

Lured by the promise of a new publishing era, Time Warner went for the deal. But hasty (over a weekend) due diligence overlooked key information: many "dot coms" of that era were already declining, the Internet "pipes" were speeding up and attracting new players, the clashing cultures of the two companies, the financials suggested that AOL was way overvalued – and doomed to decline.

The largest deal ever - and the greatest failure ever. Bad due diligence.

Hot spots
In business (including nonprofits), there are several critical areas that beg for deep due diligence. Here are some:

Hiring a new employee – add a bad employee into a key position and the cost is significant. Hiring, training, and onboarding costs. Potential damage done to the organization. Plus the cost of replacement can be two-three times the salary.

Selecting a poor vendor – contract with a key supplier who cannot perform and the expense can be overpowering. Poor products, late deliveries, irritated and lost customers, dents in your reputation.

Big order from a nasty customer – if the purchaser is over-demanding, a late payer, harasses your staff, complains constantly, abuses your products, and bad mouths you, is it worth it? Not if you wind up losing money on the deal.

Moving into the wrong facility – you get stuck with a long-term contract for a space that is expensive to operate and maintain, has limited use, and is being circled by a bad neighborhood. Big trouble, time drain, and significant expense.

Untargeted marketing campaign – your marketing gurus set up a broad, expensive advertising effort with little matching of your product and an intended audience. Wasted time and money, and an opening for your competitors.

In every one of these examples, solid due diligence might have reduced risk.

Avoid flames of failure

Due diligence is defining areas of risk, assessing impacts, and determining plans to mitigate risks. It is about leadership demanding due diligence and then absorbing the findings. Before making critical decisions.

Don't cut corners. The cost of good due diligence will be far less than the potential damage done by inadequate investigation. Sometimes it is prudent to use outside resources to perform good due diligence. Take time. Do it right.

There are available templates of information needed for adequate due diligence in different situations. Also available are lists of questions to ask in a variety of business situations that need strong due diligence.

The bottom lines

Do due diligence. Or call it risk mitigation. Demand the use of internal and external resource to provide everything that you need to know before making key decisions. About anything important. Find the "devil in the details." Avoid fires.

LEADERSHIP LESSON 28

HOW TO CLEAN UP A TOXIC ORGANIZATION

Phew! Things are not working so well. Yet, you have some good people, a big market, strong products, no overwhelming competition, and your financial situation is ok. But conditions are getting worse. What's wrong? Likely a dysfunctional organization. Why?

Remember the adage, *"Don't let a rotten apple spoil the rest of the barrel."* One bad employee can damage an organization. As the rot spreads, several disenfranchised employees can ruin a company.

Stop the spread. Find the sources of poisoned people and either modify their behaviors or let them go. Fast.

Smell the fumes

Where is the least productive part of the organization? The root problem could be there. If some of the employees are infighting, creating drama, and trying to gain personal position – more money and status – these are indicators. These employees are not interested in the team.

Or, if the bad apples are unethical, being manipulative and annoying, then this is more evidence. And they might be blaming others for their own poor performance. Worse, they are taking credit for the good work of others.

These are toxic employees spreading dysfunctional rot into an otherwise good organization. Wake up.

The stench of failure

There could be bullying. Good employees might not speak up about the issues if they think they will be called "whistleblowers." Some of the best employees may leave for a better work environment. Pathetically, the bad apples will stay. Comfortably.

Some good remaining employees might develop physical and emotional issues. They can be torn between wanting their jobs and income, yet sick of the toxic work environment.

Time is running out. Leadership must step in and resolve the issues before good employees and customers leave. And, once part of the organization is sick, the entire company can become infected.

Fumigating the area

You don't need to terminate anyone – yet. Here are ten practical and proven ways to neutralize the spreading toxins:

1. Use internal and external HR resources to eliminate bad behaviors.
2. Hold informative meetings to describe specific negative actions.
3. Don't identify offenders by name in public; do it privately if necessary.
4. Include all leaders and managers in these sessions.
5. Describe the pain and cost of behaviors that are ruining the organization.
6. Articulate the value of open communications and respect for others.
7. Incentivize people to become team-based and support the organization.
8. Reward those who exemplify the right kind of behaviors.
9. Offer professional counseling to help appropriate individuals.
10. Continue rebuilding the organization with programs for improvement.

Yes, in the end terminate those who will not or cannot change. Make room for promotions and new hires that will help create a healthy, well-functioning team.

Oh, oh

What if top management is the poison? It happens. Blockbuster Video failed because of boardroom infighting over how to do a strategic deal with Netflix. Blockbuster gone. Netflix thriving. By the way, "toxic leader" is an oxymoron: a true leader cannot be toxic. Real leaders find, cure, and prevent toxicity.

The bottom lines
Smell trouble. Something stinks when everything seems to be ok, but the business is sliding. Look for toxicity in the organization. One or more bad employees may be poisoning others. Find out where the problem is and implement a plan to neutralize it. Quickly. Then smell the roses.

LEADERSHIP LESSON 29

DISCOVER THE POWER OF SERENDIPITOUS LEADERSHIP

The "aha" moment. A discovery of unexpected good. Miraculous. A stroke of grace. And you were not even looking for it. An unanticipated order for significant business. The new perfect employee just shows up. A product problem simply disappears. Blind luck against all odds? Beyond luck. Call it serendipity.

Serendipity: when a positive effect occurs with no seeming cause. It just happens in completely unexplained ways. Always a welcome surprise. Even when it is something that helps us avoid a disaster.

Good leaders somehow recognize and seize serendipitous moments. How?

Google it
In 1997, within the first year of Google's startup, founders Sergei Brin and Larry Page decided to choose between continuing their new company or pursuing their Ph.D. degrees at Stanford University.

They decided to go after their doctoral degrees and tried to sell their new search engine to Yahoo and others for $1 million. All potential buyers, including Yahoo, declined. So, Brin and Page decided to stick with the formation of Google.

Seventeen years later, Google is a $66B global company with 60,000 employees, generating exceptional products and profits. And one of the best companies in the world to work for. Serendipity.

Grab it

Serendipitous events may be occurring all of the time. All around us. Every one of us can relate at least one significant occurrence of something wonderful that happened in our business careers. Something that "came out of the blue." And we were not looking for it.

But what happens when we ARE looking for serendipity? Something changes. More of it shows up more often, and at a higher intensity. We are not looking for something specific, but we are tuned into a channel of infinite possibilities.

Why did Howard Schultz grab a cup of espresso in a Milan, Italy coffee house and serendipitously realize that great coffee houses were as much (or more) about good social places to meet as good coffee beans? This led to Shultz buying out a fledgling coffee shop called Starbucks and turning it into the steaming king of coffee. Serendipity.

Serendipitous leaders

Leaders who cultivate serendipity have some common characteristics that we all recognize, want, and can achieve:

- Open to all possibilities at any time.
- Anticipating good things "just around the corner."
- Creative intent about transforming good things into better things.
- Holding positive thoughts about their business and organization.
- Caring for people and wanting good things for them.
- Intuitive about knowing when to seize a serendipitous moment.
- Global view in seeing how something in one place can work in another place.
- Instincts that see through perceived barriers.

Above all, they have a spiritually based belief in some power beyond human limits. George Washington called it "Divine Providence."

Cultivating the field

Get this. Quantum physics describes the Universe as a "field of all possibilities." Serendipitous leaders seem to attract good things from this field. They observe some well-known practices that include: daily prayer and meditation; reflection; journaling; exercise; deep breathing and relaxation; time with family and friends; reading uplifting books and articles. And humor with gut-busting laughter!

The bottom lines

Eureka! You found it. An unexpected happy discovery just occurred. And you had nothing to do with it. Serendipity. Great leaders have common characteristics and practices that attract serendipity. Enter the field of all possibilities. Be a serendipitous leader.

LEADERSHIP LESSON 30

WHAT DO YOU KNOW ABOUT THEORY M LEADERSHIP?

Theory X? Theory Y? Theory Z? All are defined styles and methods of leadership and management. X and Y were born by academia in the 1960's, largely out of MIT's Sloan School of Business. Z was popularized in the 1980's, stemming from Japanese management ideas. These leadership models are still around, more or less. But with questionable long-term results.

Theory X
X supposes that workers generally dislike their work, and have little inherent motivation to perform well. So, heavy rules, instructions, and monitoring are key to meeting organizational goals. Yet, unwanted side effects can be a culture of constraint, distrust, low creativity, and ignoring employee potential. Maximum control. Centralized management.

Theory Y
Y proposes that most people perform well in reasonable working environments. Workers become satisfied from their intellectual

and physical activities. And they are responsible with creative solutions to problems. Leaders see employees as mature and work with them in participatory, self-governing ways. But things can get sloppy. Minimum control. Decentralized leadership.

Theory X+Y
The proponents of Theory X and Y finally understood that the context and environment of a given workplace should determine whether leadership style X or Y should apply. In practice both are used according to a given situation. Applied dynamically.

Theory Z
During the 1980's explosion of Japanese manufacturing excellence and global influence, Theory Z was born and it worked for a while. It focused on the strong loyalty of employees to the organization. "Jobs for life" was a mantra, with the well-being of employees as a centerpiece – both on and off the job. Z leadership and management prompted high levels of satisfaction and productivity. In a paradoxical play, American corporations copied the Japanese. And became more competitive.

And then ...
Many companies proved that Theories X, Y, and Z could work – more or less. But, the more recent onslaught of global competition, the Internet rewiring of the world, and a rewiring of corporate values toward compensation for executives, board members, and shareholders opened up some questions about Theories X, Y, and Z. Do they really work? One answer is, "not so much." More than 50% of U.S. workers want out of their jobs. Now what?

Theory M

Mentoring. Contemporary leaders and managers are becoming mentors to their employees. This trend began with the advent of "servant leaders," taught by educator Robert Greenleaf in the 1970's. Happy employees make happy customers. The organization succeeds: employees and all stakeholders.

The "Mentoring Leader" in action is the story of Southwest Airlines. 35 continuous years of continuous profitability while other airlines floundered.

What are the key characteristics of mentoring leaders? They:

- Take personal interest in employees to help them be successful.
- Help employees advance their careers.
- Build powerful, collaborative, and durable teams.
- Provide dynamic influence on an as-needed basis.
- Do not view employees as "underlings," but as symbiotic partners.
- View employees individually without forcing them to be the same.
- Empower all employees to be their very best.

More proof? Southwest has had no layoffs, while competitors let tens of thousands go.

The bottom lines

Be a mentoring leader. Take a personal individual interest in employees and their success. Ask all leaders and managers in the organization to do the same. View employees as partners in success. Empower them to be their best. Don't wait.

LEADERSHIP LESSON 31

THREE STEPS TO ACHIEVING LEGACY LEADERSHIP

Endowment. This is what the best leaders leave behind them. Not their values – these are the qualities that supported their leadership. Not their personalities – those define their distinctive interpersonal style. Not their accomplishments – that is the record what they did. Now the question is, what did we really receive from them? What inheritance did they give us? Their bequest?

Legacy leaders intend to create something of lasting value for others. They are generous givers and are not focused on just generating monetary wealth.

They leave three lasting legacies: indelible visions, durable teams, stellar products.

Step #1 – Visions that stick

Sweeping, sustained visions dominate the viewpoint of legacy leaders. These visions are so powerful that they engage others to build entire, new industries. Amazon has created an online shopping bulldozer that has forever changed the landscape of the retail shopping industry.

Founder Jeff Bezos saw this possibility in 1994 – just as the Internet began to wire the world. Simultaneously, he saw an ancient book industry as the first target. Now, it is not just books. Amazon sells 2 billion different items from 2 million vendors.

This indelible vision continues. More things to buy, more ways to buy them, and more ways to deliver them. Millions of customers well served. Globally.

Step #2 – Teams that stay

Legacy leaders attract and retain great talent. The key word is "retain." Long after these leaders are gone, large percentages of the teams stay as part of the go-forward organization. This is intentional, not accidental.

Microsoft founder, Bill Gates, built a legacy team that took the business from a garage to a giant. It changed the face of computers and information technology Computers in our offices, in our homes, in our hands.

When Gates vacated the CEO seat he had a strong organization in place, including his replacement. Steve Balmer continued to orchestrate the ongoing success of Microsoft. A durable team.

Step #3 – Products that shine on

How many companies can we list who produce one great product and then faltered? More than those who succeed with streams of products. Legacy leaders make certain that this does not happen. They and their teams create an ongoing future product roadmap that outlines an unending succession of great products.

Apple Computer, both under founder Steve Jobs and now continued by his successor, Tim Cook, has provided a relentless stream of computer hardware, software, and systems that dazzle its buying audience.

Products that are feature-rich, easy to use, and sleek to handle. Stellar stuff.

Altruism all around

Bezos, Gates, and Jobs have lived as legacy leaders. They have been less interested in personal fame and fortune – and more focused on developing valuable legacies for the world around them: indelible visions, durable teams, stellar products. Good for employees, customers, our world. And us.

Yes, they did receive fame and fortune – but as a byproduct of their legacy leadership. Not as an end unto itself. Never.

> *"Leadership is about making others better as a result of your presence and making sure that impact lasts in your absence."*
>
> – SHERYL SANDBERG, COO OF FACEBOOK

The bottom lines

Decide now. What is the enduring legacy that you will leave for our world? Not your values, personality, or reputation. Leave three things: indelible visions, durable teams, and stellar products. These serve others. For good.

LEADERSHIP LESSON 32

HOW TO OPEN THE GIFT OF A BAD DECISION

Really? We'd rather not make a bad decision. But it sometimes happens for reasons we could have controlled. We have some options: ignore the poor decision and keep going anyway; go down a different path and hope for better; relabel it as a mistake. Or learn something useful from the bad decision. Really.

Running away from poor decisions leaves "something on the table" because the value of learning good lessons is ignored. Lessons for the future.

Simply turning to a new direction with no learning allows the same bad decision to be repeated. Insanity.

Bad decision or big mistake?
Too often we re-label a bad decision as a big mistake. Purchasing a bad product is a mistake. Failing to research the product before

buying it is a bad decision. A mistake is made without an intention. A decision is made with intention, even if the outcome is not good.

When we mislabel our poor decisions as mistakes, we might feel better. It takes away our sense of responsibility. Maybe we can blame someone else.

The better choice is to learn something useful from our bad choices. How?

Appreciative inquiry

Here are a few ideas to learn effectively from bad decisions:

Do it soon – examine the decision and its consequences before it is forgotten.
Blame no one – invite a trusted team into a meeting where it is safe to be open.
Ask revealing questions – including …

- What was our objective?
- What did we fail to know beforehand?
- What other solutions could we have used?
- What are the three most important things we have learned?
- How would we do it differently in the future?

Capture these inputs – and share with others so that more people in the organization can learn how to make better decisions.

Red flags
Can we avoid bad decisions? Likely not. But we can do some things to minimize them. There are warning signals that suggest we might be making a bad choice:

"*This decision will make me happy or someone else happy.*" If that is the case, all logic behind the decision is being thrown aside and the organization (and you) might be very unhappy. Soon.

"*This decision must be made right away by me, and I don't need help.*" Would a little more time help create a better decision? Endless research proves that group decisions are far better than individual decisions. Ask your team for help.

"*I would rather ask for forgiveness than for permission.*" If a bad decision is too costly for the organization, forgiveness won't matter. You might be fired. Permission can be fast if you have good logic for your decision. Documented.

Recovery
If it is possible to recover the ball after a fumble, these actions might help: claim full responsibility, be honest, make no excuses, take steps to move forward; avoid making the same mistake again; apologize, explain, share what you have realized, don't beat yourself up; refocus on the present, grab the positive, ditch the negative; go proactive, make fixes and changes now.

The bottom lines
Bummer. We made a bad decision. Don't ignore it, but work with the team to learn from it. Also learn the red flags that suggest we are about to make a bad decision. Recover from poor choices quickly. Don't repeat them. Ever.

LEADERSHIP LESSON 33

HOW A LEADERSHIP REBOOT CAN HELP YOUR ORGANIZATION

Slowing down? If you are, your organization might be, too. Businesses and nonprofits tend to take on the tenor of the leader. Customers and prospects might sense it as well. We are like computers: we slow down or become ill. Time to refresh yourself. And the rest of the system – your organization. Click "reboot."

Take a rest. Check out for a little while. Self-care is essential to good leadership, management, and individual contribution. Refresh your screen of perception.

> *"Rest when you're weary. Refresh and renew yourself, your body, your mind, and your spirit. Then get back to work."*
>
> *– Ralph Marston*

Power down

Before regenerating your business, organization, or team, focus on regaining your own footing. Here are some proven ways to reset you:

Relax: take some time off; go on a long weekend mini-vacation; take a long, hot shower or sit in a hot tub; unwind.

Breathe: find an easy chair; inhale and exhale long, slow breaths; spend 20 minutes twice a day doing this. Too busy? Spend 30 minutes twice a day; stop thinking.

Exercise: work out; practice yoga, ride a bike several miles at a good pace, jog, run, walk, or use an indoor treadmill; play tennis or racquetball; sweat.

Eat: wholesome food; consume less more often; walk afterward; suppress sugar carbs; curb fat; keep water accessible and drink it frequently; stay hydrated.

Sleep: cut caffeine, especially late day; have a good mattress and pillow; sleep in a cool room; kill noise; wake up and go to bed at the same time every day; take cat naps.

Read: kill the business books for now; read a good book about self-care; find humorous articles; read about your hobbies and avocations.

Do these things daily, not just weekly, monthly, or annually. It is your operating system. Then reboot your teams.

Restart the system

Copy and paste your recharged self to your team. When we are feeling upbeat both physically and emotionally, it is easier to boost our organization.

Here are some successful ways to regenerate and energize an organization:

Prioritize: review and recalibrate workloads; look at plans and programs to see if they still make sense; ask your organization about ideas for what's important.

Communicate: increase the level of your communications with your people; foster more communications throughout the organization; share successes and concerns frequently.

Create: find exciting new projects to build the business forward; have a challenging project that attracts your best people; introduce unique new products into your markets.

Serve: be a servant leader; treat employees as your number one resource; support and mentor them; build trust; make them happy and they will make happy customers.

Simplify: strive to reduce and eliminate all complexity; free the team to be more productive; streamline processes; MIS – make it simple, KIS – keep it simple.

Laugh: fun increases productivity, develops creativity, expands learning, strengthens relationships, builds teamwork, creates opportunities, prompts creativity and, yes, enhances leadership.

When you are recharged, it is easier to recharge your organization. And, you get further energized from a winning team. Power up!

The Bottom Lines
Reboot yourself. Learn and practice good self-care. Get your mind off business and onto relaxation. When you are recharged, it is a good time to recharge your team. Look at ways to be a better leader. Reboot your organization.

LEADERSHIP LESSON 34

WHY "ANTICIPATED SATISFACTION" IS THE CORE OF GREAT MARKETING

Anticipation. That upbeat feeling that arises from imagining forthcoming satisfaction. We may not want what someone is selling. But we purchase products and services based upon both logic and emotion. And, emotion tends to rule. We buy anticipated satisfactions. We'll feel better after we buy it feelings.

Remember the hit song by Carly Simon, *"Anticipation,"* with a lyric ... *"chasing after some finer day."* Smart marketing people know this. They craft marketing and sales messages that appeal to our anticipated satisfactions.

And this is why we see, hear, and read pre-announcements, teasers, and trailers. We imagine the satisfaction we'll get by purchasing whatever is being offered.

I'll have another Apple, please

Apple is a master of selling anticipated satisfaction. Apple's advertising and PR ignites our need to be fulfilled. And they send out a barrage of teasers – ads that let us know a great new product is coming. Coated with how we will feel when we have it in our hands, desks, and purses. We can hardly wait. For the next Igottahavit.

CBS, Disney, and others in the entertainment industry leave a trail of trailers, clips of forthcoming shows that leave us suspended and salivating before they arrive – sometimes six months from now. Can't wait to see it.

Toyota became the automotive Godzilla in a huge way when they used the famous tag line, *"Oh what a feeling!"* We went for an emotional ride well before we took our new Camry out for a spin.

B2B too

Don't get the idea that we are dealing only with consumer purchases. Business-to-business buyers might be more logical in their purchases. But they succumb to anticipated satisfactions as well. In a multi-million-dollar IT system purchase there are good logical reasons in a well-made decision.

Yet business buyers have the same emotions that personal consumers have. So, they, too, experience anticipated satisfactions from their purchases. Their gratifications can include:

- Making a good purchase that saves the organization time and capital
- Serving the greatest good of the company
- Getting ahead of a competitor
- Being rewarded for a good decision

- Reducing risk for the team, even if the price paid was higher
- Avoiding criticism for a bad purchase
- Feeling purposeful, successful, and valuable to the organization.

Can't get no satisfaction?

Of course good marketing teams understand the logical information that appeals to buyers: price, availability, features, functions, human interfaces, underlying science, durability, service, appearance, and more. Lots more.

Marketing leaders, both in-house employees and outside consultants, know how to research and understand the buying motives of prospects and customers – both consumer and business buyers.

The list of anticipated "satisfiers" (beyond the logical ones) begin with some aspect of happiness. Or at least the perception of happiness. These include: first to own one; improving an organization; looking better physically; fitting in; feeling safe; attracting others; intelligence; demonstrating affluence; perfection; getting noticed; trend setter; being right.

O.D. on it

> *"There are some days when I think I'm going to die from an overdose of satisfaction."*
>
> – SALVADOR DALI

The bottom lines
It's an inside job. Find out what the anticipated satisfactions are for buyers. Both business and personal consumers. Meet their logical needs. Then appeal to their emotional needs. Plus leak new product information and start attracting potential purchasers. With added anticipated satisfactions. Fulfilling.

LEADERSHIP LESSON 35

EMPLOYEES: BURN AND CHURN, OR TRAIN AND RETAIN?

Lose a good employee? One that voluntarily quit? Go figure. Figure the total cost of the loss and you will not likely want to lose another good person. Truth: the cost of employee retention is less than the cost of replacing them. Much less. Look at the facts.

Fact one: the average wage of a U.S. employee is approximately $50,000. Fact two: voluntary termination is above 10% per year. Fact three: the average total cost of replacing an employee ranges from 25% to 250% of their base salary, depending upon their role.

This price is too high for a high-performing employee. Painfully.

So, give us an alternative?
If the average cost of replacing a good employee is 50% of $50,000, then the cost is $25,000 per average voluntary turnover.

If you lose only 10 good people out of 100, that is $250,000 off your bottom line. 150% of a $150,000 employee = $225,000 alone.

Compare that to the possibility of investing in each employee to retain them. What if you were to set aside a budget for employee retention? In the above example, invest the $250,000 potential loss in all 100 employees to help keep them. That is $2,500 for every employee.

How would you spend it?

Good leaders know the answer

A solid employee retention program can be constructed with multiple parts. Here are some proven suggestions:

Flexible Hours – insist upon some fixed hours while allowing some alternative hours to create a schedule that works for both the employee and organization, relieve pressure.

Adaptable Days – give appropriate employees to the opportunity to work some days at home and expect other days to be spent in the office, cut commuting stress.

Increased Benefits – add some vacation hours, increase medical benefits, provide workout and other health benefit opportunities.

Enhanced Training – help employees expand their knowledge, offer in-house training, help pay for community college and university courses, help their productivity.

Career Development – establish potential progression of responsibilities in the organization; give a greater sense of purpose, Increase motivation.

Expressed Appreciation – tell every employee how much you appreciate them, recognize individuals for their extra effort with some gift cards, improve loyalty.

There is more ...

Non-cash Incentives – recognize that employees value their quality of life, provide some non-cash incentives such as pay for a nice dinner out for them and their family.

No Surprises – avoid shocking employees via rumor mills and company newsletters that might impact them; tell them yourself as much as possible, even by live streaming.

Get Inputs – employees feel valued when they are asked for their ideas and inputs, especially when they are asked in-person about plans, projects, and challenges.

Birthday Time – send a personal birthday card to employees and add a gift card for a coffee house (and add enough for a cupcake, too); a little means a lot.

Cash, Too – sure it is great to give good employees cash; consider keeping their salaries slightly above the market rate, and think about cash performance bonuses.

P.S. Happy employees build happy customers. Repeat customers.

The bottom lines
Figure it out. The cost of retaining good employees is less than the cost of retaining them. Far less. Build a budget just for keeping good employees. Don't unwittingly feed high performing people to competitors. Everyone is more satisfied. You, too.

LEADERSHIP LESSON 36

WHY AUTHENTICITY IS THE IRRESISTIBLE ATTRACTION OF GREAT BUSINESS LEADERS

Get real. Be authentic. It is magnetic and attracts more authentic people to us. The kinds of people we want as employees, customers, investors, suppliers, and community members. The more we reveal our true inner self as real leaders, managers, and employees, the stronger we become. People want to be around us. The kind we want to do business with. Real people.

Shakespeare knew this when he wrote, *"Above all, to your own self be true. And then as night follows day, you cannot be false to anyone."* Expose yourself.

Authenticity energizes a magnetic attraction and inspires like-minded people.

Who are we, really?
How do we know when we are being authentic? We exist, think, speak, and act from our heart and soul – our true inner self. Our

qualities and character emit honesty, integrity, and openness. We are seen as trusting and trustworthy.

It takes some courage to be authentic in business because we become vulnerable when we allow our often-protected inner self to be visible. But the rewards of established soul-to-soul, heart-to-heart connections can be enormous.

Authenticity does not answer the question of, "Who am I?" Authenticity affirms who I am. Others get it.

Will the real leaders please stand up?

Authentic leaders share the risk and challenges with their teams. They "walk their talk:"

- Warren Buffett invested 90% of his personal savings to start his top-performing investment company, Berkshire-Hathaway.
- During a 1970 recession HP employees took a 10% pay cut – including cofounder Bill Hewlett.
- In the early years of Charles Schwab & Co. the founder dropped everything to answer busy phone lines in customer service.
- Sam Walton, Wal-Mart founder, rented compact cars and checked into inexpensive hotels when traveling. Just like his employees.
- When visiting McDonald's restaurants, founder Ray Kroc picked up wastepaper in the parking lot to demonstrate that constant cleanliness is everyone's job.

Another key behavior of authentic leaders is making certain their actions consistently reinforce the one or two most important values they hold up for their organizations:

- Jeff Bezos at Amazon put customers first, sacrificing short-term profits by cutting prices, taking sharp hits from Wall Street's stock analysts. Until recently. Now he is a financial hero to his investors.
- Herb Kelleher, cofounder of Southwest Airlines', put his employees first. He never laid his people off even as competitors let tens of thousands go. Southwest is continuously profitable.

Authentic leaders do not wander off their walk. Not ever.

Open up

So, how do we become more authentic? Some common suggestions are: seek our inner voice and pay attention to it; match our thoughts, words, actions at all times; daily meditation is a common practice; reflective journaling of our day; serving others; exercise; a good diet. Self-care.

Some symptoms of successful growth in authenticity include: developing a sixth sense, an intuitive knowing; increased interest in others, feeling grounded, even when stressed; feeling "goose bumps" when authentic others say something that resonates with us; more humor. And, it is easier for us to enroll others in our work.

The superficial can excite; the authentic can inspire.

The bottom lines
Be real. Authenticity attracts and inspires like-minded people. Great business leaders know and demonstrate this. Pay attention to your inner voice and amplify authenticity. Like attracts like. Build and lead authentic teams. Build good business.

LEADERSHIP LESSON 37

SEE HOW CLARITY IS THE LENS OF LEADERSHIP

Confused, muddled, ambiguous? Clarity is seeing things transparently in all areas of the organization and its business: vision, mission, values, objectives, strategy, actions, communications. You name it. When one or more of these essential business elements is not crystal clear, anything can happen. Or nothing can happen. The windows of opportunity need washing. Quickly.

Successful leaders ask often, "Is this clear to you?" When there are too many responses of, "No," it is time to clarify as much as possible to everyone possible.

> "What will become compellingly important is absolute clarity of shared purpose and set of principles ... that every member of the organization understands in a common way, and with deep conviction."
>
> — DEE HOCK, FOUNDER/CEO OF THE VISA CREDIT CARD SYSTEM

Questions of insight

Another question to ask is, "What about this is not clear?" Then listen. Carefully. And, "Tell me what about how to improve the clarity of this for you and others." Take notes.

Anytime is a good time to set eyes on clarity. An especially good time is when preparing and reviewing plans: strategic plans, business plans, and other plans. Clear plans are the path to clear actions.

Don't wait to be asked. If something anyone communicates is not clear, tell them and offer to help them have more clarity. You owe it to yourself and others.

Transparent communications

We are a race of communicators in a communications race. Not just speaking and listening, reading and understanding, but through a bigger barrage of communication conduits: telephone, text, email, social media, video, broadcasts and podcasts. And more.

Clarity – is the foundation of effective communications. It embraces additional elements of clear messages to employees, customers, prospects, vendors, and communities: context, content, color, and carrier.

Context – why is the message being sent and what are the surrounding factors, conditions and environment? A clear explanation about the purpose of the message is important.

Content – what is the message, what does it convey in facts and feelings, and what is the intended call-to-action for the reader? The content must be quickly and efficiently delivered to the intended audience without unclear meaning.

Color - who looks at the message and what do they need to see or hear for maximum attraction to the information being conveyed? Interesting fonts, graphics, colors, photos and sounds that clarify the message and engage recipients are powerful.

Carrier – where does the message move from, in one or more media, to best reach the intended audience? The nature of both the message and the intended audience determines good choices of new media or traditional media as the carrier.

Got clarity?

Opacity is the opposite of clarity. Lack of clarity breeds distrust, disbelief, gossip, corporate conspiracy, and low teamwork. These kill organizations.

Integrity, trust, and teamwork are built upon open, honest, transparent, clear communications at every level. Getting clear magnifies trust, helps create simple solutions, provides acceptable accountability, and helps decision-making. Faster.

The best leaders have clarity in many ways, including:

- Clarity of vision, mission, values, goals, strategies, actions.
- Clarity of the organization and business.
- Clarity of what created sustainable success.

The bottom lines

Get clear. Ask questions so that everyone understands clearly the organization's plans and actions. Insist that every aspect of all communications with everyone embrace clarity. Seek clarity with everyone and everything. Now, do you see?

LEADERSHIP LESSON 38

FIVE PATHS TO PROFITS FROM AUDACIOUS VALUE STRATEGIES

Value? Who gets the value? You mean customers are not the only ones who benefit from good value? Definitely. While a major strategic focus is on strong gains for customers, some companies place plenty of emphasis on shareholder value. And this is not the end of the benefit buffet. Others hunger for value.

Who else wants and deserves good value? Employees, communities, and (really?) vendors. Strong organizations profit from creating value for all stakeholders. Strategically.

Would you go so far as to create value for a competitor? Maybe. Read on.

1. Customer value
The genesis of value. The buyer gets something for the price they pay. When that purchase has equal or greater worth – now or in the future – than the worth of the payment, the buyer experiences

high value. And vice-versa. Value is like beauty; it is in the eye of the beholder. Perception.

Example: Apple Computer – even at higher prices, customers have given Apple stunning profits and $200 billion cash on hand, more than any tech corporation.

2. Shareholder value
Hello, Wall Street. Investors want a good return for what they spend to obtain shares in a company. And, the leadership of those companies return value to their investors by growing the company's financial worth. "The Market," amplified by analysts, often determines perceived value – vs. the real current and longer term projected future financial worth of the company. Thank you, Warren Buffet.

Example: Berkshire Hathaway – proof that value-based investing pays off with a 20% average return per year to shareholders vs. 10% for the S&P over 49 years.

3. Employee value
Yes, employees are called increasingly, "human assets." Wise leaders understand the true worth of employees beyond simply a pool of working robots. Successful leaders practice "servant leadership" by seeing good employees as the hub of the organization. Happy employees build happy customers. These leaders create high value for employees: meaningful engagement, great working conditions, humane management, trust and teamwork, excellent benefits. Results? Customer value and shareholder value.

Example: Southwest Airlines – 30+ years of continuous profitability with an amazingly low employee turnover of 2%.

4. Community value

Give back. Organizations hire employees and attract customers from the surrounding community. Grateful companies make certain that they are providing value back to the community. In several creative ways: helping fund community social services, hiring the disadvantaged, supporting local education, participating in festivities, paying taxes fairly. In turn, the community supports the company. More value for everyone. Partnership.

Example: Target Corporation – since 1946, Target has given 5% of profits to their communities, now $4 million per week, for education, health, and more.

5. Vendor value

Wise organizations create good value for their good vendors: win-win pricing, healthy relationships, long-term planning, true partnerships.

Example: Amazon has 2 million vendors providing 2 billion items. Whew!

P.S.

Astute leaders develop value among competitors. Example: "Auto Row" where all auto dealers co-locate on a given street and do cooperative advertising for the good of all. Industry associations act similarly, e.g. The American Banking Association. Cooperation among competitors. "Coopetition." Value for all.

The bottom lines
Create value. Strategic value. For all stakeholders, not just some. The total worth of the organization and it business is the sum of all value created for customers, shareholders, employees, communities, vendors, and others. Great leaders do it.

LEADERSHIP LESSON 39

WHY BREAKING BREAD IS SO GOOD FOR BUSINESS

Food. Meetings. Stirred together they are a satisfying mix for building business.

Businesses have been taking clients out to lunch or dinner since restaurants began with the French Revolution. A time to relax, relate, and reveal our reasons for doing business. Beyond simply filling up with food, the French word *restaurer* means to restore. Oui.

Sharing food in a business setting restores our energy and restores the human connection. Eating together sets a table for deeper discussion of issues and ideas, and warms the soul. Shared food has a welcoming, hospitable nature.

Spirits are lifted (yes, in a wine glass, too), trust and integrity are amplified. Pass the bread, please.

> *"Food is something holy. It's about sharing. It's about honesty. It's about identity."*
>
> – Louise Fresco, scientist, food activist, Stanford University professor

A buffet of means

Going out to restaurants is only one way to partake. Other methods include having food brought into the organization by employees, caterers and restaurants deliver food, or an in-house cafeteria or dining room can provide the edibles.

Smaller organizations might ask employees to bring their own brown bags for a luncheon meeting. Potluck food is a popular way to go, too.

Sometimes simple stuff is just as effective. Snacks and finger food can create the same positive effect as a more elaborate meal.

Food for thought

The power of shared food can be effective in a wide range of possibilities:

- Meetings with prospects to discuss opportunities.
- Sessions with customers to resolve concerns.
- Planning meetings around new strategies, products and services.

- Employee assemblies to share news, build morale, and enhance teamwork.
- Board meetings with directors and advisors.
- Recognition and reward rallies to honor excellent employees.
- Meetings with vendors to hone good working relationships.
- Picnics and other outings for employees and their families.
- Goodbye time for good employees who are moving away.

Whenever and wherever there is a reason for people to get together, good food gives good vibes.

Chew on this

Free stuff. Many companies in the fast and furious hi tech industries (and others) provide kitchens loaded with free food – breakfast, lunch, snacks, and sometimes dinner. Sure, it is usually simple items, boxed, frozen, fresh fruit and vegetables, make-your-own ingredients. Junk food for those who must.

Employees can work more effectively and sometimes longer when they must, or want to, or both. Rush hour traffic can be avoided. And employees save money – appreciatively.

Eat at the desk, or in a conference room family style. Use the sink to clean up afterward. Just like at home.

Digest this

Google and Facebook are among the companies that provide free food to their employees. It is effective because those companies have positive cultures and work environments. A Harris Poll survey finds that 30% of employees like free food as part of their overall workplace happiness.

Hallmark operates a company-subsidized cafeteria at low cost to employees. And they recognize the value of serving delicious and healthy food.

An additional survey notes that the powerful combo of food with teambuilding helps build a strong positive workplace culture.

The bottom lines
Got food? An essential way to build better business is good food. In meetings of all kinds. With employees and all kinds of people. Food helps bond us, fosters integrity and trust, and boosts work effectiveness. Eat up!

LEADERSHIP LESSON 40

HOW TO AVOID THE CUSTOMERS YOU NEVER WANT

Customer always right? Nope. Particularly the poisonous ones that make leaders and employees mentally, physically, spiritually sick. They include the customers who provide no profits, a stream of unwarranted complaints, and take a staggering amount of time to manage.

Turn the same (or less) amount of energy into finding great new customers. And taking very good care of existing customers who deserve your best efforts.

Clue. Avoid taking on toxic customers in the first place. Figure it out when they are poisonous prospects. Run away.

Their stripes
The "Field Guide of Poisonous Customers" identifies the following characteristics of customers (and prospects) to stay clear of:

- Their clocks run at high speed. Everything is an emergency or an urgent request. You and your team run full out to meet their demands. And your other customers get less service from you. Slow them down or charge them more.
- Changing their minds – over and over. They cannot be satisfied. Constant reworking of paper work, product exchanges (resulting in plenty of unsellable goods for you to burden). All of this at your original price. Once, OK. More than once, no way.
- They may initially look quite normal. Nice and friendly, too. You might start giving them a lot of extra time, products, discounts, and services. They might not be grateful, then start expecting the freebies, and ultimately demand everything. Just say, "No" or let them go.
- Indecisiveness. They never seem to make up their minds, constantly ask for revisions of proposals and orders, and take long periods of time to decide. Some never decide. Back away.
- You lose. Given all the lost time, inefficiencies, low morale, and other costs, your profit margin has shrunk to low, none, or a loss. Your return on investment, including sweat, is miserable. Create a win-win with these customers, or pull out. Professionally and promptly.
- Your team goes nuts. Constant, urgent, unreasonable, sometimes nasty demands shove even mild-mannered employees to the boiling and blowup point. You risk losing good employees. If the situation cannot be changed, do not fire your employees. Fire the customer.

Toxic customers can badmouth your organization in the marketplace. Likely, 20% of your customers cause 80% of your problems – the ones to fix or fire and replace. And, they may flaunt, "I will sue you if I don't get my way." Call their bluff.

Oh, and they rarely pay on time. Convinced?

Last call

Do what you can to salvage the better of noxious customers. Have a heart to heart talk, outline new guidelines for the relationship, start billing for rush activities, tighten up contracts, and charge for revisions.

They won't accept your changes? This is a perfect signal that you need to let them go. Most likely, they will treat another vendor the same way – perhaps your competitor.

The tradeoff truth is that you will find better customers to fill the void. And your team will have more time to find them. And serve them well. It's a win-win.

The bottom lines

Seller beware. Learn to identify noxious customers (and prospects). Professionally, but firmly, attempt to enforce a fair, win-win relationship. Else, run away from poisonous prospects, and walk away from contaminated customers. Use your energy to serve your good customers – and find more of them. De-stress the team. And yourself.

LEADERSHIP LESSON 41

HOW DO SUCCESSFUL LEADERS START THEIR MORNINGS?

No snooze button on the alarm. Great leaders activate themselves and their teams starting first thing in the morning. Personally and professionally, men and women. Even those who are not "morning people" have a routine that starts earlier rather than later. And there is a persistent pattern. Organized.

Power up
They are early risers. In time to greet spouses, children, and other household members, including pets. Having breakfast together with conversations about "What's up for you today?" is important.

Most prefer a healthy, nutritional breakfast – even if it is fast. And those leaders tend to drink a lot of water throughout the day.

Many leaders arise early enough to work out at home or nearby before breakfast. An aerobic sweat relieves and prevents stress. Another stress managing and mind-clearing routine for some is morning meditation time.

On the road again
Getting to work opens opportunities for a fast start. If by car, strong leaders listen to audio books. They are life-long learners to improve their leadership skills. Some will handle early phone calls (hands free, of course).

If traveling by bus, train, and air, many will read and handle business related files of information. More digital, less paper.

The point is that true leaders maximize their mornings for a better business day.

Point of order
The majority of excellent leaders begin their days with a prioritized list of the most important activities and actions for them and their teams. Some items are follow-ups on decisions and actions. Other things in the list are new. All are must-do's on the priority list. Few are want-to-do's. None are nice-to-do's.

A sampling suggests that the best leaders keep this list short. It contains both broad strategic actions and near-term tactical activities.

The key question is, "Will each item in the list contribute to a substantive improvement in the business?"

Kickoff time
Either at the office, or by remote audio/visual meeting systems, leaders start the day with a fast check-in for their team. The prioritized list is discussed, agreement is gained, and actions assigned.

Some leaders hold a longer staff meeting on Monday's to dispel the "Monday morning blues," and get the team focused on the positive opportunities of the week ahead. A great week. Then, individual sessions with staff members is normal – and necessary.

Get to work, everyone.

Practices make perfect

There is more. Other leaders have additional practices they use at the start of their workday, including:

- Greet others in the organization with their name and a smile.
- Add to a daily journal and gratitude list, read some past pages.
- Visualize success with dreams, purpose, and goals.
- Get on the phone for a few minutes with a good mentor.
- Get organized, clear the desk, and communicate with an assistant.
- Read an inspiring article or pages from a book.
- Leave time for unexpected events because they will happen.
- Take on toughest challenges first.
- Kill unimportant, non-urgent emails.
- Communicate some useful news to the organization.

Opportunities are like sunrises. If you wait too long, you miss them.

– WILLIAM ARTHUR WARD

The bottom lines

Kill the alarm. Get up, work out, greet family, eat a good breakfast. Get to work. Prioritize the day, communicate with the team, and take action. Use early hours productively. Get inspired and give inspiration. Be grateful. Have a great day.

LEADERSHIP LESSON 42

THE ART AND SCIENCE OF GRATITUDE IN BUSINESS

When to be grateful in business? Always. It is easy to forget being grateful. Yet there are so many to thank. Not just customers: employees, peers, management, suppliers, and the surrounding community. Why? Gratitude builds customer loyalty, strengthens organizations, and uplifts everyone involved. Builds better business. That's a lot.

Don't forget to be grateful to family and friends who support your career, job, and work.

And remember to recognize and be grateful for all the mentors – academic and business – that helped you get where you are. But this is not the end of the list.

Gratitude journaling

Psychology researchers offer a big buffet of tools to help us be happy. At the top of their long list is a gratitude journal. Per the *Journal of Personality and Social Psychology,* people who keep weekly gratitude journals have a greater sense of well-being, fewer health issues, and are more optimistic about each coming week.

More good news. People who keep gratitude lists are more likely to make progress with key goals, according to a *Georgia Psychological Association* report.

Get a notebook and write everything you are grateful for about your work, weekly. Why not daily? And don't forget to read it. Often.

The hard part

Being grateful for adversity is a mark of maturity. It is the tough stuff that spurs our growth: emotional, mental, and spiritual. For we learn just as much from our mistakes as we do from success. Maybe more.

> *Mistakes are the best teachers. One does not learn from success. It is desirable to learn vicariously from other people's failures, but it gets much more firmly seared in when they are your own.*
>
> – MOHNISH PABRAI, INDIA-AMERICA, BUSINESSMAN, AUTHOR

So learn to be grateful, too, for the errors that teach us indelible and invaluable lessons.

Pumping endorphins

Think pumping iron and working out is the only way to fill your body with your own built-in antidepressant, anti-anxiety "pill?"

Gratitude releases our endorphins into the bloodstream, suppresses excess adrenalin, and makes us and others feel fantastic. Get grateful.

Got gratitude?
Be grateful that you can be grateful. Because most people are not. According to a *University of California at Berkley* survey:

- Only 52% of women and 44% of men express gratitude on a regular basis.
- Just 49% regularly express gratitude to their spouse, 37% to their children.
- 20% express gratitude daily to their parents, 15% to their close friends.

Punch line: a mere 10% express thankfulness to their colleagues at work and 7% to their boss or employer. What an opportunity for improvement!

Expressing gratitude
Head-felt gratitude says, "Thanks." Heartfelt gratitude says, "Thank you so very much. I appreciate you and your business … or your thoughtfulness … or your great work."

90% of Americans believe in prayer. A blessing is a prayer of gratitude that wishes good for the receiver. Perhaps this is why we often hear, including in business, "Bless you."

Other forms of gratitude can be a smile, a phone call, text, email, and handwritten notes. Small gifts, an extra measure of goods and services work, too. Give some.

The bottom lines
Get grateful. Thank as many people in your workplace as possible. Customers, employees, prospects, peers, management, suppliers. Strengthen your organization and business. Increase your sense of well-being. Thank you so very much – everybody.

LEADERSHIP LESSON 43

BYE-BYE BUSINESS PLAN, HELLO BUSINESS MODEL

Chao. You served us well, old business plan. But you are clunky, wordy, and overweight. And the business world changes so fast that we spend more time keeping you updated than utilizing you to plan our future. Now what?

Add the business model. It describes how to maximize profits from products and services. And that is the very core of a business plan. The guts.

Business models evolved in the early 1900's. A classic example of one type of business model is to sell the razor at no profit and then sell compatible, high-profit razor blades. Forever.

Tell more ...
So what is contained in the business model? A conventional template for a good model was defined in 2008 by Alexander Osterwalder. The *Business Model Canvas* is a visual chart that depicts the key elements of the business, including:

- Key Partners – buy/sell relationships, including strategic relationships, joint ventures.
- Key Activities – high priority actions to implement the value proposition; e.g., developing robotic production to reduce costs.
- Key Resources – what is needed to develop value for customers; e.g., human, intellectual, financial, facilities.
- Value Propositions – products and services that meet customer needs; e.g., uniqueness, newness, price, usability.
- Customer Relationships – essential type of interaction with customers; automated service, self-service, personal assistance.
- Channels – main method of distribution to customers; e.g., retail, wholesale, distributors, agents.
- Customer Segments – what group are the customer in; e.g. mass market, niche
- Cost Structure – important monetary considerations; e.g., cost-driven, economies of scale, fixed and variable costs.
- Revenue Streams – how to generate income from customer segments; selling goods, subscriptions, advertising fees, licenses.

You can see good visual representations of the business model canvas at http://www.businessmodelgeneration.com/downloads/business_model_canvas_poster.pdf or https://canvanizer.com.

Who uses business models? Major organizations including Microsoft, MasterCard, Adobe, 3M, Intel, Deloitte, Oracle, Xerox, Intuit. And many others.

Examples of business models

While the razor and razor blade model was an early example, there are now many variations of business models. Here are some, including how they monetize their products and services:

Affiliate Model – someone sells a product and collects commissions.

Bait and Hook Model – give a product away and then sell supplies for it.

Freemium Model – give something away in exchange for contact info.

Direct Sales Model – bypass distributors and sell direct to customers.

Low-Cost Model – sell something at low cost and then sell profitable upgrades.

Auction Model – sell something to the highest bidder.

Pay as You Go Model – sell for usage of a service.

Recurring Revenue Model – long-term service contracts with periodic renewals.

Advertising Model – give information away and sell advertising.

Franchise Model – replicate a business and license it to others.

There are many more business models, but all of them describe the essence of the business – how to realize profits from the sale of products. Maximum profits.

Is the business plan really dead?

No, but it is changing. Today's business plans are much shorter and to the point. And, the business model now becomes the centerpiece of the business plan. The brief business plan is the outer wrapper of the heart of the business – the business model.

The bottom lines
Put it aside. But, don't throw out your business plan. Instead, create a good business model. It is the guts of your business – maximizing profits from products. Then, build your brief business plan around a good business model. Smart business.

LEADERSHIP LESSON 44

WHY CONTEXT IS THE FRAMEWORK FOR SUCCESSFUL LEADERSHIP

Wait. "That statement was taken out of context." Or, "Please describe the context for our proposal." Context. Typically we do not describe the context for what we think, communicate, and do. This creates confusion. What is context, really?

Clues. Here are some alternative words for context: the setting, clarification of meaning, circumstances, conditions, factors, state of affairs, situation, background, scene, setting, frame of reference. Framework.

Analogy: the framework of a building is the support for the rest of the structure. No framework, messy building. No context, messy leadership.

Let's put it in context
"We just got an order for $200,000 worth of our XYZ product." Sound good? Maybe. What if the context were:

- It is the only order this quarter, it is the end of the quarter, and the sales goal is $2 million.
- The order came from a customer whose business is in decline.
- There will be no profit because XYZ is too expensive to produce.

Now how does this order look?

Here is a different context for that same order of $200,000:

- It is our first order on the first day of a new quarter.
- XYZ is a new product, great potential in a large market, highly profitable
- Our sales goal for XYZ this quarter is $1 million.

Does this sound more exciting, given the context?

Context for our ideas, words, and actions is crucial for leaders – and everyone.

Contextual leadership

Clearly leadership in action must first address a circumstance, a situation – the context. This is the ground of meaningful dialog and decisions. The framework.

And, there is a larger picture. It extends beyond any given circumstance. It embraces an entire organization across longer periods of time. It is the general situation. And the context includes the industry, the market, nature of the business, people, finances, and culture – every element of a business. Even in nonprofit organizations.

Matching of leadership qualifications and style is paramount. A good match leads to accelerated growth and sustainable success. Bad match? Trouble.

Contrasting contexts

No organizational leadership context is exactly the same. What is the context of a given company or organization?

- Optimizing an existing business?
- Building a new product line?
- Divesting the business or part of it?
- Acquiring other businesses?
- Accelerating organizational development?

Just because leaders are great a particular situation, does not mean that they will succeed in another.

Samsung's CEO, Kun-Hee Lee, was significantly successful with electronics. So he decided to do the same with automobiles. He invested $5 billion in an already oversaturated auto market and failed. Why? A radically different context.

Both Steve Bennett and Tom Rogers succeeded at General Electric. Later, Bennett generated a whopping 60.9% annualized rate of return during his first three years at Intuit. But Rogers produced a -30.2% annualized return over three years at Primedia. The difference? Not management skill, but adaptation to a new context. Skillfully.

Steve Jobs succeeded at Apple, then was a success at Pixar, and later wildly succeeded again in a different situation back at Apple. Jobs was contextually portable.

The bottom lines
Stop. First get the context of a given situation, organization, or company. Then, decide what needs to be done. If you do not fit the context, let someone else lead. No one size fits all. The shoe must fit the context of the foot. Comfortably.

LEADERSHIP LESSON 45

IMPROVISATION: WHEN YOUR PLAN ISN'T WORKING

Something isn't clicking. Your idea is highly creative. It supports your strategic business plan. You have laid it all out, thought of everybody, everything, and everyplace. But, the gears of implementation are not meshing. Now what?

Improvise. It has been a tool for musicians and comedians. No sheet music, no script. Get some jazz musicians together and they will improvise great music. Give a comedian a surprise prop and they will make us laugh. Miles Davis did it with his trumpet. Jonathan Winters did it with anything. Even a tree twig.

True in business, too.

Improv on the job
You are making a significant presentation to a major customer or prospect. The projector fails. Improvisers will start drawing words and diagrams on a whiteboard. Or just start giving the presentation in sincere words with nothing else. The slide deck is not the presentation – you are. Authentically.

Engineering improvisation solves a problem with tools at hand. An example was the re-engineering of carbon dioxide scrubbers with the materials on hand during the Apollo 13 space mission. A save.

Sometimes improvisation produces a better result than the original plan. In the movie "Pretty Woman" actor Richard Gere presents an expensive jewel to actress Julia Roberts. As she reaches to touch the jewel, Gere abandoned the script and playfully snapped the box shut – genuinely surprising Roberts. Her laugh was so honest and the scene so good that it stayed in the film. A hit.

Can we learn to improvise?
Yes. In fact, we likely have already learned somewhat. As children we improvised some of our toys out of household items. A kitchen pan turned into a drum. In spite of mom's objections.

Improvisation is hyper-speed creativity. At our creative best we will find alternative paths to a desired result.

Organizations such as businessimprov.com teach business improvisation. They stress leadership agility, meeting uncertainty, and leveraging change.

Duke University teaches improvisation in business as an MBA elective course. An adjunct professor trained with the founders of improvisational theater.

A number of corporations have introduced improvisation via corporate training courses. Google, PepsiCo, MetLife, and McKinsey & Company are among them. Improved team building and communications are among the benefits realized.

Improvisation as a process

In any business situation there is some common goal to be met expediently. Improvisation is a stepped process to meet that goal. Here are some steps:

Learn
Pay attention and learn everything possible about a challenging business situation. Use all your senses. No analysis. No judgment. Just get information.

Agree
Understand and accept the situation as it is without trying to control it. Use the facts as fuel for decisions to be made.

Integrate
Take what is known and mix in creativity. Abandon old solutions and generate new ones. Quickly try and test. Solidify and amplify what works.

Communicate
Work closely with an ensemble of people to get more ideas, suggestions, and resources that will quickly amplify and accelerate a solution.

This process is about "out of the box" thinking. Or "no box."

The Bottom Lines

Plans can fail. When it happens, improvise. We did it as children for play. Now we do it in business for success. Get help and learn how to improvise "out of the box." Be agile and thrive in uncertainty and change. Improvisation is at work.

LEADERSHIP LESSON 46

BUSINESS BULLY, PEOPLE MANIPULATOR, OR POSITIVE INFLUENCER?

Give it up. A so-called leader, manager or anyone who verbally and emotionally bulldozes employees and others are unworthy of their position. Ditto manipulating people with lies and half-truths to get what the manipulator wants. Demanding and dishonest. Both.

Unfortunately, there have been a few "tough guys" who have built financial empires, but the moats around them are littered with decomposed self-worth. Recently, major media has identified a number of well-known corporate leaders who value profits more than people.

"Everybody's gonna get rich" was the rallying glue that held most of the human capital in place. De-humanized capital. Is there a better way? Read on.

Throw the book at 'em

Dale Carnegie's book, that is. Carnegie, an American writer, lecturer, and developer of famous courses in self-improvement and interpersonal communication skills, wrote a bestselling book.

In 1936 he published, *How to Win Friends and Influence People*. It became a perennial bestseller and continues to rank among the top 40 self-help books of all time. It is about people – first, foremost, and always.

Warren Buffet, among the wealthiest business people globally, said, "It changed my life." How?

It is all a matter of words
Words are powerful. They can scar people for life – or they can raise us up into higher planes of potential. Professionally and personally. Quickly.

Carnegie summarized his book in four key areas: basic ways for us to interface with people; the means to have others like us; attracting others to our ideas; how to lead – how to change people without offending them or causing resentments.

And our words can be spoken, written, emailed, texted, phoned, posted in social media, delivered by facial expressions and body language.

Interfacing with others
It's simple:

- Do not complain, condemn, or criticize.
- Appreciate others in sincere, authentic, positive, and honest ways.
- Create in others an eager want for what you provide.

Approaches to cause others to like us
Honestly be interested in other people. Wear a smile as much as possible. Remember people's names and use them often. Ask others to talk about themselves and genuinely listen. Communicate to the other person's interests. Sincerely help the other person to feel important.

Attracting others to support our ideas
Twelve tenants:

1. Avoid arguments.
2. Respect others' opinions without saying, "You're wrong."
3. When you err, admit it immediately and emphatically.
4. Begin communications in a friendly way.
5. Ask questions to which others will answer, "Yes."
6. Allow others to do most of the talking.
7. Let others feel your idea is his or hers.
8. Honestly see things from others' points of view.
9. Be empathetic with others' ideas and needs.
10. Appeal to higher motives.
11. Elaborate your ideas.
12. Offer a friendly, positive challenge.

Lead by changing others' thinking without offense nor resentments
Start with praise and authentic appreciation. Indirectly point out others' errors. Tell about out your own mistakes without referencing the other person. Instead of giving direct orders, ask questions. Always let others save face. Acknowledge every improvement.

Model positive behaviors for others to adopt. Provide encouragement. Make mistakes seem easy to correct.

The Bottom Lines

Don't bully others. Or manipulate them. Use honest approaches to interface with others, cause others to like us, attract others to our ideas, and lead by changing others' thinking. Authentically influence others. It is easier. And durable.

LEADERSHIP LESSON 47

SYNCHRONICITY IN BUSINESS: WHY GOOD THINGS HAPPEN FOR NO REASON

Amazing! Can't explain it. "We were one order short of reaching our monthly goal and received a huge, profitable order 'out of the blue' without ever making a sales call." "I saw a business book protruding from a bookstore shelf, bought it, returned to my office, and then saw a copy of it on my managers' desk." "I was thinking about calling an important business contact and in a few moments they called me." What is going on?

Have you ever had this kind of thing happen in your business experience? Most of us have. But we cannot explain it statistically in human terms. No way.

Dear Dr. Jung
In the 1950's the well-known Swiss psychologist, Dr. Carl Jung, coined a new word – *synchronicity*. He was describing the simultaneous occurrence of events that appear to be significantly related, but have no discernible causal connection.

Leaders and organizations that recognize and act upon the emergence of these events based upon synchronicity are shaping the future.

Synchronicity in business is a growing area of interest. A classic book on the subject is "Synchronicity: The Inner Path of Leadership." Author Joseph Jaworski, son of the Watergate trial judge, Leon Jaworski, explains synchronicity in the context of leadership.

Expect synchronicity

To Carl Jung's point, synchronicity events occur without our conscious effort. If the concept of "synchronicity" seems strange, there are other similar notions that can convey a similar idea: grace, serendipity, extra-sensory perception (ESP), miracles, divine providence, and being in The Flow." It's a spiritual thing.

Regardless of what you might call it, what if you could anticipate, expect, attract, and welcome more of these remarkable transactions – for the benefit of your organization and yourself?

This possibility is real. Follow along.

Attract synchronicity

Here are some ways to cultivate more synchronicity. Stay in the present moment, be authentic, and allow your intuition to help guide you:

- Reserve some quiet time to allow a spontaneous idea to emerge. Be open to a new, non-preconceived idea. It will appear.

- Believe in your idea with a feeling that it will have a positive effect on you and your organization.
- Give shape to the idea by visualizing a positive result from implementing the idea. See how the idea can actually work.
- Ponder the idea, share it with others, and get some feedback. Often, input from others will enhance the idea.
- Spend time to clarify how the new idea can be implemented. Feel what it would be like to have the idea working perfectly.
- Allow the idea to rest – let go of it.
- And when the inner "nudge" happens, act upon the idea.

These are the conditions in which synchronicity breeds and births. The time from inception of the idea until it happens with strong confirmation can be a few stunning seconds – or longer, but still stunning. Beyond statistical understanding.

University interest
Northern Arizona University provides a fascinating research paper, "Teaching Spiritual Synchronicity in a Business Leadership Class." You can read it at http://franke.nau.edu/search/synchronicity. Numerous other universities now teach various aspect of spirituality in business. How synchronous.

The bottom lines
Don't freak out. When simultaneous business events occur that are significantly related and have no discernible causal connection, it is synchronicity at work. Expect, anticipate, and attract synchronicity for better business. Amazing!

LEADERSHIP LESSON 48

THE MAGIC OF MUSIC IN OUR WORKPLACES

Not a new song. Music is decidedly effective in the workplace. It's a spiritual thing. Workers labored to chants and drumbeats long ago. 19th-century handloom workers sang folk songs. Britain provided music for workers via radio in the 1940's. Research in 1972 found that factory employees were more productive when they listened to upbeat music. Sound right?

More recently, MusicWorks surveyed 1,000 small-medium business owners and learned that 77% said that music boosts morale, 65% indicated that music increases productivity, and 40% noted that it increases sales.

And, as children we heard Snow White's Seven Dwarfs, "Whistle While You Work." Listen up.

Corporations, too

Music can have positive impacts for individual employees and groups across the entire business – directly impacting their mood and happiness. Music can unite employees and create a bond that unifies the organization. It can help synchronize team actions and output (proven with soccer teams). Get rhythm.

Oh, and music reduces stress. Studies indicate that 40 million Americans who suffer from exaggerated worry and tension are six times more likely to be hospitalized. Cost? $300 billion annually. Kaiser-Permanente is a forerunner in advocating music for health, using it effectively in its own healthcare company.

Get music and get well. At less cost.

Where is that sound coming from?
It's everywhere. Retail stores, airline terminals, and more. Restaurants are rampant with music (sometimes so loud we cannot converse). Specific music is chosen to help set the mood: a relaxed buying mood, a rushed "eat and get out" staccato, and music to wait by. Everywhere.

Wise organizations play appropriate background music. Certain organizations will benefit from upbeat music that promotes safe and effective production. Other groups may play music that amplifies creativity.

Today, employees are largely allowed to play their own music from mobile devices through earphones – if their productivity is OK. Or better than OK.

A few notes
Music can help balance our brains. The right side of the brain is best at:

- Pattern recognition, music, art, and images
- Expressing and reading emotions
- Intuition and creativity

Our left side of the brain is adept at:

- Logic, reasoning, and analytical thinking
- Language
- Numbers

Better brain balance helps the whole person be a better employee – or leader.

Some music accelerates learning and creativity, according to a classic book by Dr. Don Campbell. A former professor of music at the University of California at Irvine, his book is, *"The Mozart Effect."*

Einstein credits some of his ideas to inspiration he received by listening to Mozart. His violin is viewed as an important tool in his problem-solving kit. He attributed his scientific insight and intuition primarily to music. Imagine.

Melodious sounds send calming dopamine into the reward area of the brain, just like eating a delicacy, looking at something appealing, or smelling a pleasant aroma, said Dr. Amit Sood, a physician of integrative medicine at Mayo Clinic.

Sood also notes that our minds tend to wander, particularly when we are unhappy. Good music brings us back to focus on the present moment.

> *"Music can change the world because music changes people."*
>
> – Bono

The bottom lines

Let the music begin. Consider the dramatic results from good music at work. Background music for everyone. Personal music for employees. Enhance health, happiness, creativity, and productivity. Lift up spirits. Listen to the music.

LEADERSHIP LESSON 49

WHO MUZZLED WORD OF MOUTH MARKETING?

WOM. Word of mouth. Nobody killed it. In fact, as a marketing tool it is very much alive and growing. Before any form of print, radio and television advertising, there was only word of mouth. Face-to-face WOM was amplified by the telephone. And now the Internet plays a role – telling a friend about a product via email and social media. Why is word of mouth so powerful? Trust.

Get this: per Nielsen ratings, 92% of consumers believe friends over all forms of paid advertising. Period.

And 64% of marketing executives believe word of mouth is the most effective form of marketing. But, only 6% indicate they have mastered WOM. Opportunity!

Free marketing
When someone tells another about good products and services, the marketing cost is effectively zero. However, getting that chain reaction started does require some marketing work and cost.

It might take significant advertising and publicity in one or more forms to secure your initial and ongoing buyers. Asking for an order is a standard method of selling. But, why not ask your customers to tell others, too?

Faberge cosmetics long had an advertising tag line, "Tell two friends." It worked.

Hello internet

Word of mouth might sound quieter today because social media has quickly become one of its channels. The use of Facebook, LinkedIn, Yelp, and others is a radical expansion of WOM. It is easier, faster, and less expensive for someone to tell another about a pleasant (or unpleasant) experience with a product. And it can be enhanced with audio/video. Then it is not so quiet!

Powerful statistics:

- 85% of brand-fans recommend good brands to others via social media (Sycapse).
- 43% of consumers are more likely to purchase a new product when learning about it on Facebook (Nielsen).

Belief in paid advertising is declining. Growth of social media WOM is exploding. Trust this.

WOMMA?

Word of mouth marketing even has its own association. WOMMA. The Word of Mouth Marketing Association at www.womma.org. Key members include American Express, Google, Honda,

Consumer Reports, DuPont, IBM, Motorola, Nissan, educational organizations, and others. This is big business. Seriously.

And, WOM is not just about consumer products – it plays a very powerful role in business purchases. You can hear it now. "We just installed an amazing new IT system from Godzilla Computers. It is far better than anything we have ever had. You should take a look at one."

Amazing proof:

- 91% of business purchases is influenced by word of mouth (USM).
- 61% of IT purchases are most influenced by word of mouth recommendations (B2B Magazine).
- 56% of business-to-business purchases are impacted by direct WOM, 88% via online WOM (BaseOne).

Example

Ericsson pioneered cellphones with embedded digital cameras. They struggled with traditional ways to excite customers. So, they used 60 actors in major cities that posed as tourists, asking strangers to take their picture. The strangers were handed the new cell-camera, along with an enthusiastic education about how to use it. Afterward, the strangers talked up their experience with others. Sales took off. WOM won.

The bottom lines

Tell a friend. Word of mouth (WOM) remains the most effective form of advertising. Why? Buyers trust the experience of people they know. WOM is essentially free and can be fanned out rapidly via the Internet. Spread the word.

LEADERSHIP LESSON 50

IMPORTANT STUFF TO KNOW ABOUT GOALS AND OBJECTIVES

Subtle or significant differences? Goals and objectives are related, but distinctly different. And their distinction is important for leaders, managers, and individuals. Too often we think goals and objectives are the same. They are not. Their differences are essential to good planning. There is more.

Goals are broad expressions of desired, primary outcomes. Objectives are measurable steps to achieve goals. Goals and objectives have differing timeframes, and intended effects.

Oh, one more thing: goals feed strategies and objectives fuel actions. Intrigued?

As seen from above

Here are some top-down perspectives about goals and objectives – their similarities and differences:

Goals embrace the purpose of directed activities.
Objectives are something that actions are intended to specifically accomplish.

Goals are more generic actions – outcomes for which we work.
Objectives are more specific and support achieving the intended, associated goal.

Goals are usually not measurable or tangible.
Objectives are both tangible and specifically measurable.

Goals have longer timeframes.
Objectives are mid-shorter term.

Examples:
Goal: we will succeed in our industry and do what no organization done before.
Objective: we will complete $10million of new financing by the end of this quarter.

Their kin: strategies and actions
Why have goals and objectives without approaches (strategies) and tools (actions) to accomplish them? Otherwise, we can splatter ourselves against the Wall of Try instead of crossing the Bridge of Success. Here goes.

Strategies are the general paths we follow to attain related goals. Strategies answer the question of "what" to do in a field of possibilities, which is littered with landmines of limited resources, creative competitors, and the fast clocks of change.

Actions are the methods and tools we utilize in pursuing objectives. They answer the question of "how?" These can involve processes, people, products, and more. Actions are defined in terms of "who, where, and when?"

Confused?

All together now

Here is an example for the interrelationship of goals and objectives, strategies and actions:

- Goal: be a leading supplier of our Widget-A product in sales revenues.
- Strategy: convince buyers that our Widget-A product is the market best by partnering with leading retailers.
- Objective: capture over 50% of the global market for Widget-A's in five years, according to the annual Forbes Widget Market Report.
- Action: through creative marketing campaigns, leverage our retail partners' brand awareness programs to include focused messages about Widget-A's.

The goal states a purpose for the actions, is a generic outcome, not easily measured, and it has an implied longer timeframe. The strategy sets a general direction to attain the goal. The objective establishes a specific target, is measurable, supports the goal and strategy, and is relatively short term. And, the action describes how to pursue the objective.

It all tightly ties together for success. Nicely.

Look north
Vancouver, Canada is rated by Fast Company and others as among the top ten North American cities in a variety of categories. Vancouver recently developed an aggressive business plan with 10 key goals, accompanying strategies, measurable objectives, and specific actions to expand its presence as a major global city: http://vancouver.ca/files/cov/corporate-business-plan.pdf

The bottom lines
Plan. Decide where you are going from here (unless you want to stay put). Else, carefully state your goals, construct supportive strategies, outline collaborating objectives, and list high priority actions. Get moving. Keep moving. Succeed.

LEADERSHIP LESSON 51

WHEN AND HOW TO FIRE YOURSELF

Had enough? Leaders, managers, executives, individuals, owners, entrepreneurs, and board members often resign by their own choice. Even in good times. And good times may be the best time for a change. Or, bad times might be the best timeframe for others. Your choice.

The signals and symptoms for change are usually "in the air." Right in front of us.

Our feelings and intuition play a key role when it is time to move on. First, the question of "why" needs be examined in a realistic way.

Now take action – and the key questions are "when" and "how?"

Conditions are crucial
The good. You are successful, you have helped an organization improve and thrive, and you are recognized for your contributions. You have every reason to be satisfied. So why quit?

The bad. You are unable to succeed no matter what, you are far better than you can currently show, and you have tried everything to progress – but cannot. You are even well liked and well paid. What is wrong?

The ugly. You feel pending doom, the organization is failing, rumors are rumbling, and even good people who are leaving are not being replaced. What is going on?

The "why?"

Here are some possible reasons, signals and symptoms, about why you want to make a change. You …

- Are bored and ready for something more stimulating
- Want to be in a different work environment.
- Would like to turn your business over to someone else with new skills.
- Desire to move and be closer to family or in a different geography.
- Need to rest for a while, then go back to work.
- Want to change your career or type of work.
- Retirement or semi-retirement is now attractive.
- Wish to turn your job over to someone else who has additional strengths.
- Interested in taking a lesser position elsewhere.
- Feel underutilized and want to grow.
- Dislike management.

And even more reasons. You …

- Are underpaid.
- Do not feel recognized or rewarded.
- Are pushed to work harder and longer and feel like a machine.
- Want to spend more time with my family and friends.
- See that your company is old and stodgy, and in a declining industry.
- Do work that you do not like.
- Cannot get promoted and are in a dead end situation.
- Want to work part time.
- Are not asked for input and are not listened to.
- Question your company's ethics.
- Cannot trust others in your environment.

Time for a change?

The "when" and "how"

First, lay out your exit plan with all the steps, milestones, and dates. Base this plan upon why you are leaving and what is your desired end point, no matter what it is.

Start a quiet, methodical search to find your next opportunity before quit your current role. Alternatively, if you have the financial resources, quit, get some rest, then do a thorough search for your next role. Take the initiative in managing your change.

"Change brings opportunity."

– NIDO QUBEIN, AMERICAN BUSINESSMAN AND UNIVERSITY PRESIDENT.

The bottom lines
Decide. Get moving. Understand why you want to leave your current role. Observe the signals and symptoms. And, know everything about your intended new role. Lay out your plan and commit to follow it. Take a deep breath. Act.

LEADERSHIP LESSON 52

HOW GREAT MANAGERS CAN BECOME GREAT LEADERS

They are not the same. Managers and leaders have some common characteristics, many different qualities, and significant behavioral differences. Often, good leaders are good managers, too. More often, good managers are not good leaders, even if they want to be. Unless they learn how. How?

Forget the idea that all good leaders are born with leadership instincts. Only a few at best – and even they must further develop it. By learning. Just like most solid leaders do through university and other courses.

After that, there are books galore and OJT (on the job training). And more.

Contrasting characteristics

An essential learning tool about many things – including management and leadership – is to contrast their similarities and differences. A famous Claremont University management guru gave us a good start:

> *"Managers do things right. Leaders do the right thing."*
>
> – PETER DRUCKER

And, there are many more contrasts from a variety of sources:

- Managers follow the vision. Leaders create and communicate the vision.
- Managers manage processes. Leaders lead people.
- Managers take the next step. Leaders take the first step.
- Managers ask "how" and "when." Leaders ask "why" and "what."
- Managers organize people. Leaders align people.
- Managers administrate and control. Leaders motivate and inspire.
- Managers coach, tell, and push. Leaders mentor, teach, and demonstrate.
- Managers' work with the status quo. Leaders challenge the status quo.
- Managers coordinate resources. Leaders unleash potential.

Many managers can learn and practice leadership characteristics, qualities, and behaviors. A transformation from manager to leader is possible.

Qualified qualities

Managers have many of the following qualities: mental, rational, consultative, persistent, problem resolution, intent, analytical, structured, deliberate, authoritative, stabilizing, power by position.

Leaders have most of the following qualities: soulful, visionary, passionate, creative, flexible, inspiring, innovative, courageous, imaginative, experimental, initiating, personal power.

Basic behaviors
Managers behave by doing things right, focusing on how things should be done, conforming and controlling, are rules-oriented and transactional, ensuring stability of the system, pursuing procedures and objectives, and managing change.

Leaders behave by doing the right things, focusing on what can be accomplished, exhibiting innovation, making commitments, ensuring outcomes, being transformational, energizing the system, pursuing vision and inspiration, and creating change.

Much more
Managers administrate, are non-unique, maintain, focus on systems and structure, inspire, control, have short term perspectives, eye the bottom line, imitate, live in the status quo, and are a classic good soldier.

Leaders innovate, are an original, develop, focus on people, inspire trust, have long term perspectives, eye the horizon, originate, live in challenging the status quo, and are a classic good general.

Elegant example
Warren Buffett is among the three wealthiest people in the world. But, his first business ventures included selling chewing gum, selling weekly magazines door-to-door, delivering newspapers, and detailing cars. Next, he managed investment sales, security analysis, and stock brokering. Finally, he invested his own savings to

start his existing investment company, Berkshire Hathaway, Inc., and continues to lead it today. Today, his net worth is over $65 billion. Now he is a leader.

The bottom lines

Great managers. They are essential to good business. But, they might not be leaders. Yet, if they successfully learn and practice the characteristics, qualities, and behaviors of great leaders – a transformation can happen. Great leaders.

HOW TO ORDER MORE BOOKS

The author, Tom Zender, hopes that you enjoyed this book.

Additional copies of both books in this series by Tom Zender are available:

The Bottom Lines 2016: 52 Unforgettable Lessons in Leadership

The Bottom Lines 2017: 52 More Motivating Lessons in Leadership

They can be ordered at www.amazon.com in both the paper and digital e-book versions.

Tom Zender
tomzender@me.com
www.tomzendermentor.com